The Russian Revolution 1917–1921

BERYL WILLIAMS

Basil Blackwell

Copyright © Beryl Williams 1987

First published 1987

Basil Blackwell Ltd
108 Cowley Road, Oxford, OX4 1JF, UK

Basil Blackwell Inc.
432 Park Avenue South, Suite 1503
New York, NY 10016, USA

British Library Cataloguing in Publication Data
Williams, Beryl
   The Russian Revolution, 1917–1921.——
   (Historical Association studies).
   1.   Soviet Union——History——Revolution,
   1917–1921   2. Soviet Union——Politics
   and   government——1917–1936
   I.   Title II. Series
   947.084'1   DK265

   ISBN 0–631–15083–8

Library of Congress Cataloging in Publication Data
Williams, Beryl
   The Russian Revolution, 1917–1921.

   (Historical Association studies)
   1. Soviet Union——History——Revolution, 1917–1921.
I. Title. II. Series.
DK265.W484 1987   947.084'1   87–15088
ISBN 0–631–15083–8 (pbk.)

Typeset in 11 on 12pt Baskerville
by Photo·graphics, Honiton, Devon
Printed in Great Britain by Page Bros. (Norwich) Ltd

Contents

Introduction

In February 1914 P. N. Durnovo, a former Minister of Internal Affairs and a leading member of the State Council (Russia's upper house), submitted a memorandum to Tsar Nicholas II. In it he warned that a war with Germany would be 'mortally dangerous both for Russia and Germany, no matter who wins ... there must inevitably break out in the defeated country a social revolution which ... will spread to the country of the victor' (Golder, 1927, p. 19). His advice, and the prophetic picture he painted, went unheeded. Other voices were pressing for a determined stand against the threat of German aggression. In any case, when war broke out it was widely believed that Russia had no option but to participate. The fate of Serbia was of real consequence to St Petersburg if Russia's interests in the Balkans were not to be abandoned, and her role in the alliance system meant that non-participation would end her status as a European Great Power.

The Russian army had been reformed and modernized since the defeat by Japan in 1905, and enormous sums had been spent on the navy. Nevertheless the War Office warned that war was a viable option for the regime only if it could be over within six months; but this was a common delusion of the governments of Europe in 1914. The internal situation was near crisis point that summer, and many opponents of tsarism believed a revolutionary situation was imminent. Despite the precedent of the

1

Russo-Japanese war, some voices in court circles still argued that a short war and the accompanying patriotism would benefit the government.

The monarchy had survived the revolution of 1905 by a mixture of concessions and repression. By June 1907, when the new Premier, P. A. Stolypin, restricted the franchise to the newly created state Duma, or parliament, most of the more liberal concessions had already been withdrawn. It was clear that the government, unlike the Kadets (Constitutional Democrats) who had dominated the first Duma, did not envisage its transformation into a western-type parliament. Stolypin wanted administrative and legal reforms to be achieved by working with a conservative Duma within the framework of a modernized autocracy. Reform was, however, to be balanced by repression, and he failed to get support even from the conservative nobility of the third Duma. By his assassination in 1911 all that he had managed to achieve from his wider plans was a peasant reform.

The attempt to invest the peasantry with individual private property in land, to break up the village commune with its common land tenure and to encourage an enclosure movement and capitalist smallholdings had two purposes. One was to create a class of small landowners who, with a growing industrialist class, would provide the monarchy with a new base of support. The other was to encourage these new, richer peasants to grow for the market and to provide, in their turn, a market for manufactured goods. In practice Stolypin's reform failed to transform the Russian countryside. Those 'separators' who left the commune suffered from debt, rising land prices and social isolation. Relatively few peasants actually established independent smallholdings, and 60 per cent of peasant families were still in the commune in 1917.

Nevertheless there was no threat of peasant revolt in 1914. Although the black earth belt of central Russia, which suffered most from poverty and overpopulation, clung to traditional practices, other areas did not. The peasantry of the south-west and the north-west adapted well to the new market opportunities provided by urbanization and the international grain trade, even if often within the commune rather than outside it. Easier mobility also enabled the towns to grow rapidly between 1906 and 1914. Better primary education, imported western goods, a freer press and the cinema were beginning to develop a more European and politically aware urban population. The Duma had little power, but its debates were reported in the newspapers, and it served as a forum for public opinion. Russia was changing in the decade before the revolution, but arguably in ways not conducive to the stability of the monarchy.

In 1913 agriculture still absorbed 45 per cent of the national income and modern industries remained islands in a predominantly rural economy. It was, however, the threat of urban discontent that caused tsarist ministers to worry about the future. Strikes had been a feature of urban life since the 1890s and had reached the scale of a major movement during the revolutionary years of 1905–7. After a decline during the period 1907–12, the number of strikes again rose sharply in 1912, and with it the influence of the revolutionary parties. By the summer of 1914 the strike figure for that year already stood at 3,500, the highest since 1907, and 72 per cent of them were labelled as political by the authorities. An 8 per cent industrial growth rate in the 1890s had created areas of advanced industrial technology, especially in the capital. Living conditions were bad and wages low. Trade unions and strikes were illegal before 1905.

In 1914 heavy industry was recovering slowly from an economic depression at the turn of the century and from the upheavals of 1905. Industrialists formed syndicates and appealed for more government aid, but it was the war which was to revitalize the stagnating metallurgical industries. Industrial output doubled in the capital between 1914 and 1917. The army was well, if never sufficiently, supplied until the end of 1916, when shortages of raw

3

materials, fuel and transport took their toll. It was, however, a mammoth task. The number of Russian casualties was enormous along the long front, and by 1917 over 14 million men had been mobilized. The effects on agriculture and the manufacturing sector were considerable. All transport and industrial production was geared to the needs of the army, and the civilian economy collapsed under the strain. Failure to supply the towns, especially the capital in its exposed northerly latitude, led to strikes and bread riots.

After the first round of military defeats, the army, despite bad leadership, held the front line with some credit and, although disaffected by the end of 1916, did not mutiny. It was the large urban garrisons of reservists who were to prove unreliable when faced with street disturbances and who were to identify themselves with the workers in February 1917. The urban proletariat grew rapidly during the war. According to one estimate, there was an increase from 250,000 to over 400,000 in Petrograd (as the capital, St Petersburg, was renamed in 1914). As workers were called into the army, women and young peasants flooded into the towns. By 1917, 45 per cent of all workers were employed in the armaments industry, one-third of them in government-owned factories. By the February revolution, although half of the Petrograd proletariat were experienced urbanized workers, half were not, and over one-third of workers were women or were aged under eighteen. Many of these new workers were unskilled and prone to spontaneous outbursts of disorder. It was precisely these elements which came out on to the streets of the capital in February 1917.

The effects of war, mass-production techniques, modern technology and a rapid influx of new workers into the towns at a time of inflation and shortages had succeeded, where the revolutionary movements of the nineteenth century had failed, in creating a revolutionary situation across much of Europe. Unfortunately the effects of the war meant that opposition movements in all countries were unprepared to take advantage of it. In Russia the opposition was split between liberals (Kadets and the more moderate Octobrists) hoping for legal, parliamentary change, and the revolutionaries. The Socialist Revolutionaries (SRs), heirs to the old populist movement (see Glossary), still envisaged a uniquely Russian tradition of rural socialism based on the peasant commune, and they maintained their tradition of terrorism.

The Russian Marxists (Social Democrats) had developed from the 1880s out of, and in conflict with, the populist movement. They applied Marx's interpretation of the stages of western economic development to Russia, and believed that capitalism and a large proletarian class were necessary forerunners of a socialist society. The government's industrialization programme of the 1890s seemed to provide both essentials, and the Social Democrats worked to build up support among the new industrial working class. Among themselves, however, they disagreed over how far along the capitalist road Russia had travelled, and over the methods necessary to achieve their aims. In 1903 the Russian Social Democratic Workers' Party split into Bolshevik (majority) and Menshevik (minority) factions. Most Mensheviks planned for a large working-class party and a long period of capitalist development. They envisaged co-operation with the liberals during the period of bourgeois-liberal democracy until capitalism reached its final stage and socialism would be possible. The Bolshevik leader, V. I. Lenin, argued, in contrast, that a small, professional party was necessary in conditions of tsarist autocracy. He rejected any collaboration with the liberals and, in 1905, called instead for a 'democratic dictatorship of workers and peasants' to complete the capitalist phase. Although in 1905 Lenin, unlike the Mensheviks, was not expecting the bourgeois-capitalist period to be long-lasting, he did not believe that an immediate socialist revolution was possible.

Only Leon Trotsky, at that time working independently of both Mensheviks and Bolsheviks, advocated an immediate transition to socialism. His theory of 'permanent revolution', worked out in 1905–6, argued that power should be transferred at once to the soviets (workers' strike committees formed during the revolution) and that the socialist revolution would be an all-European one.

After the setbacks following the 1905 revolution, the Marxists were again gaining ground in the factories as the war approached, and it was the radical, Bolshevik, wing which gained most. They took control of the important metal workers' union in 1913. The war divided the revolutionary parties all over Europe, and few supported Lenin's call to turn the imperialist war into a class war. In Russia as elsewhere, many voted for war credits and shelved all idea of revolution until the return of peace. The regime, however, was taking no chances, and the secret police (Okhrana) ensured that most revolutionaries spent the war in European exile, in Siberia or in prison. Lenin expressed a common fear that he would not live to see the revolution.

But the war lasted too long to save the monarchy. It also affected the political scene. With Nicholas II at the front as commander-in-chief, the court involved in sexual and political scandals around the tsar's favourite Rasputin, and no one of any standing at the head of the government, the monarchy became isolated even from aristocratic circles and those who would normally have supported it. Many intellectuals took refuge in salon life, freemasonry and spiritualism. The government's refusal to create a ministry of public confidence or to allow the Duma any say in running the war led to a paralysis among the parliamentary parties. A Progressive Block had been formed in the Duma in August 1915, uniting Kadets, Octobrists, Nationalists and the new Progressist party of the industrialists. The bloc deliberately kept its demands to a minimum and refrained from pressuring the government. The Progressist leader and some left-wing Kadets favoured a more active policy and approaches to the moderate socialists and the labour movement, but to no avail. It was left to extraparliamentary liberal bodies, like the new unions of *zemstvos* and town *dumas*, to take more positive action and to challenge the government at provincial level. Their role in war work with the sick and wounded turned them into nationwide organizations employing specialists who were often more radical than liberal and brought them into contact with wider sections of society than their parliamentary colleagues. They ran hospital trains to evacuate the wounded from the front and organized emergency health care. After 1915 they also had their own committee (Zemgor) to help channel supplies to the army. Their success during the war years was to give hope that sufficient local initiative and expertise could be available to reconstruct a democratic Russia once the revolution gave them the opportunity to do so.

1 The Provisional Government, February–October 1917

The fall of the Russian monarchy was accomplished over the ten-day period from 23 February to 4 March 1917. Ten days of popular demonstrations, political manoeuvring and army mutiny developed imperceptibly into a revolution which no one expected, planned or controlled. This is not to say that the revolution was entirely spontaneous, although it was largely so, nor that there had not been various political plots and conspiracies aimed at removing Nicholas II, if not the monarchy, over the previous year. The murder of Rasputin is, of course, the best known, but A. I. Guchkov, the Octobrist leader, had also been involved in a palace plot involving masonic and military groups, at the end of 1916. Nothing had come of this, but it showed the alienation from the monarchy felt by both the leaders of the Progressive Bloc and the army high command.

Yet the Duma, even when prorogued by Nicholas during his last days in power, had no plans to assume governmental powers and vacillated fatally throughout the revolutionary period, fearful of being arrested by loyal troops on the one hand and of the *stikhiia*, or elemental force of the masses, on the other. Its president, M. V. Rodzyanko, desired above all to preserve the dynasty and to act within the constitution. By refusing to allow the suspended Duma to continue in session, he lost it the chance of declaring itself the legitimate successor to the Romanov dynasty. Only an unofficial committee of the Duma remained sitting in the Tauride Palace to form the Provisional Government on 2 March. Its lack of legitimacy or election proved a deep embarrassment for the Kadet leader, P. N. Milyukov, if not for all his colleagues throughout the eight months of its existence.

Moreover, there was no doubt that the initiators of the revolution were the workers and the reserve troops in the capital. The politicians acted throughout in response to events. Rodzyanko and Milyukov, by trying to create a constitutional monarchy, not only alienated the Duma from the republican sympathies of the streets but also weakened the Duma committee's claim to be representing the revolution.

The revolution on the streets started on 23 February in response to the introduction in the capital of flour and bread rationing. Consequent rumours of shortages led to bread riots. A lockout at the Putilov works the day before started a protest strike which was to lead to a general strike by 25 February. International Women's Day on the 23rd was used by the strikers as an excuse for a demonstration. It also added to the already large numbers of women on the streets. All the major leaders of the revolutionary movement were in Siberia or abroad when the movement started, and certainly no political party organized the revolution, which over the days developed a momentum of its own. However, the women were not just demanding 'bread and herrings', as an unsympathetic observer put it, but also an end to the war and the overthrow of the monarchy. The Putilov works was not only one of the biggest, it was also one of the most politicized factories in the capital. Many of the striking workers were members of political parties; often they were Bolsheviks.

The local Bolshevik committee of the working-class Vyborg district of Petrograd was an active, militant and long-established cell, and it was trying to lead the workers in February. There were also unofficial revolutionary agents using German money to attempt to restart the 1916 strikes. Trotsky, writing later in his *History of the Russian Revolution*, answered his own rhetorical question as to who led the February revolution with 'conscious and tempered workers educated for the most part by the party of Lenin' (Trotsky, 1934, vol. 1, p. 171), but this is a later rationalization of a more complex picture. Local Bolshevik militants may have been involved, but they were not carrying out any coherent party policy; activists of the other revolutionary groups were also present, and none of them was really leading the crowds. Indeed, on the night of the 26th the local Bolsheviks considered trying to call off the strike movement when the Okhrana arrested known militants and the demonstration was fired on for the first time. By the following morning, however, it was clear that events had gone too far to be stopped. The first signs of insubordination by the reserve garrison had become apparent, and the Petrograd Soviet had been set up, apparently on the initiative of a group of Menshevik intellectuals, on the model of the 1905 Soviet. The Petrograd city Bolshevik leader, A. G. Shlyapnikov, promptly called for it to become a provisional revolutionary government, but this was not at all what its leaders had in mind, and he received no support from the Bolshevik Central Committee. In the early weeks of the revolution the Central Committee was reorganized by L. B. Kamenev and Josef Stalin, who had returned from exile in Siberia. They were not contemplating radical policies. Indeed, they were prepared to give conditional support to the Provisional Government, taking their cue from Lenin's 1905 position that the coming revolution would be a bourgeois one. The Bolsheviks initially had little influence on the Petrograd Soviet, but it soon became clear that the crowds would look to it rather than to the Duma committee, or to any one political party, for guidance.

Meanwhile the tsar, still refusing political concessions,

attempted to return from army headquarters at Mogilev to his family at Tsarskoe Selo outside the capital. He was prevented from doing so by the presence of revolutionary troops, and the royal train was diverted to Pskov. There, with surprising ease once the real situation in the capital was brought home to him, he abdicated for himself and for his sick son Alexei on 2 March. At the end Nicholas found it easier to give up his throne than to share power. The tsar's brother Grand Duke Michael refused the throne unless it was offered to him by a Constituent Assembly, and the newly declared Provisional Government found itself *de facto* in charge of a republic. No republic was actually declared, however, until 1 September.

When the newspapers reappeared on the streets on 5 March, Russia was informed of the nature of its new Provisional Government. It was composed, with one exception, of leading figures of the liberal parties, many linked by freemasonry ties and most having belonged to the Progressive Bloc in the last Duma. It was dominated by the Kadet party and by its leader Paul Milyukov, who became Foreign Minister. The leader of the Progressist party, the textile magnate A. I. Konovalov, became Minister for Trade and Industry, while the Octobrist leader Guchkov, who also headed the War Industries Committee, became Minister of War. Its one socialist minister, an SR, was a radical lawyer, Alexander Kerensky, appointed Minister of Justice. Although he was later to become Prime Minister, Kerensky was not, in the early days, seen as a particularly important figure in the new government. He was a leader of the Petrograd Soviet, and his decision to participate contradicted the agreed policy of that body, but it gave the first Provisional Government its one direct link to the Soviet. The new Prime Minister, however, was a compromise, brought in by Milyukov to prevent Rodzyanko's appointment. Milyukov regarded Rodzyanko as both too cautious and conservative, and too much of a personal rival, to head the new government. The new Prime Minister was Prince G. E. Lvov, who was

11

not actively involved with the Kadets but was head of the *zemstvo* union and was well known for having organized support for the war effort.

Milyukov dominated the first Provisional Government until his resignation on 2 May. Because of this dominance, and because it was his later writings in exile after the October revolution which shaped the western view of the period, there has been a tendency to identify his ideas with those of the Russian liberal movement as a whole. Milyukov was, by 1917, close to what one might describe as a classic English liberal. He and his lawyer associates on the right wing of the party were concerned to turn Russia into a formal western liberal democracy with full legal safeguards for all citizens, civil rights and a parliamentary constitution. Milyukov was the linchpin of the Kadets, but, as with all Russian parties, there were strong differences of emphasis between the left and right wings. Milyukov himself, like many other intellectuals, had moved to the right since 1905 under pressure of the reality of a revolutionary situation. Those on the right of the party tended to regard the revolution as over by early March. They were concerned to re-establish law and order and to concentrate on building a new legal and constitutional structure. In contrast, left-wing Kadets, like N. A. Nekrasov, were staunch republicans and social reformers. As such they were more prepared to collaborate with the moderate socialist parties in the Soviet. In this they were closer to the original Kadet radicalism of 1905 when the party programme had been formulated. In 1905 Milyukov himself had described party members as social reformers and considerably to the left of similar European liberal movements. The 1905 policy of 'no enemies to the left' still influenced many members of the first Provisional Government, and was supported by Konovalov and Lvov. Indeed, Prince Lvov, to Milyukov's later dismay, turned out to be more a radical populist than a liberal, and in attitude was closer to Kerensky than to Milyukov.

Thus the Provisional Government as set up early in

March, although undoubtedly liberal in its policy, was far from united. Initially, however, there was reason to hope that the general support given to it from nearly all sections of society and regions of the country would facilitate its task. In the honeymoon period of the revolution, amidst the general rejoicing in the overthrow of tsarism, even moderate liberals like Milyukov could express confidence in the people's acceptance of a democratic future and a faith in popular support for the new government. As he put it in February, 'we were elected by the Russian revolution' (Riha, 1969, p. 284). It was, after all, the only legitimacy they had. Outside the capital the acceptance was indeed swift and unconditional. In nearly all towns, power passed from the old tsarist officials to committees of public safety, mainly peacefully, although sometimes accompanied by strikes and looting. These committees were almost always multi- or non-party bodies of local progressive notables, and they were joined by representatives of the newly formed soviets or popular committees of 'the democracy', as workers and peasant representatives came to be called. In all the major towns of the empire, factory workers spontaneously elected representatives, as they had done in 1905, to form town and district soviets or councils, to represent workers' interests. They recognized the Provisional Government with enthusiasm and awaited developments.

In Petrograd the situation was more violent and more complex. Up to 2,000 people had been killed or wounded in the capital in February, and from the beginning a system of what became known as 'dual power' operated with the new government and the Petrograd Soviet. The Soviet itself made its position clear in February. As good theoretical socialists the Mensheviks and SR leaders of the Petrograd Soviet recognized the revolution as a bourgeois one, and they believed it needed liberal leadership. The Soviet saw itself as a watchdog of the revolution, a temporary organ to put pressure on the Provisional Government until a Constituent Assembly met, after which it would, presumably, disappear. Workers and soldiers might see it as a sort of proletarian parliament, but this was not the view of the intellectuals who ran it. Soviet policy, despite Kerensky, was to keep a cautious distance from the Provisional Government and to support it only in so far as it carried out policies of which the Soviet approved.

In real terms, of course, the Soviet held most of the power. Crucially, Order No. 1, issued in the first days of the revolution, gave the Soviet control of the army. Order No. 1 set up elected soldiers' committees to be represented on the Soviet, which thus, despite initial suspicion on the part of the soldiers, became a Soviet of Workers' and Soldiers' Deputies. These soldiers' committees were ordered to obey the Provisional Government only in so far as its orders did not contradict those of the Petrograd Soviet. Control of arms and military discipline were removed from officers and given to the committees. The decree was issued in haste under pressure from the troops in the capital and was issued only to troops in the Petrograd district, but it quickly spread throughout the front. Many officers came to terms with the new arrangements. Moreover, as Guchkov admitted, the government could not send a telegram without Soviet approval. The trade unions which controlled the posts, the telegraphs, the railways and the major industries recognized the authority of the Soviet. Real power was never in the hands of the Provisional Government, yet in practice in the early months there was surprisingly little disagreement between the two bodies. The demands put forward by the Soviet as a condition of its support were nearly all accepted. They included a political amnesty, civil freedoms and the rapid convocation of a Constituent Assembly. They also demanded, and got, a popular militia to replace the police, and agreement that the reserve troops who had participated in the revolution in the capital should not be disarmed or sent to the front.

The government's acceptance of these demands began a process of political consensus which was to last until April. This was possible partly because the Soviet refused to take power itself, and partly because of the importance within the first Provisional Government of the radical populists and left-wing Kadets. The Soviet's programme, in fact, was very close to that of Prince Lvov. He, and many of his associates brought into the government and the administration, were *zemstvo* men. They had campaigned for years for more local autonomy and less, much less, central government. February was truly a revolution in that the political structure was radically transformed. The authority of the old regime was dismantled or collapsed all over Russia. The police were disarmed and arrested, their headquarters burnt; prisons were opened; tsarist officials were arrested or fled. Army officers in garrison towns, although not at the front, were also removed. The Provisional Government could not have ruled by force, even if it had so desired. But a new legitimacy and basis for support had to be built up. Right-wing Kadets saw this being established through elections to a Constituent Assembly. They did, however, wish to keep some form of centralized state. Lvov and those on the left of the party had a much more populist attitude to government, as was illustrated in the crucial first few weeks. What remained of the centralized administrative system was deliberately dismantled. The secret police were abolished, together with the death penalty. Officials from the provinces who came to Petrograd asking for instructions were told by Lvov: 'this is a question of the old psychology. The Provisional Government dismissed the old governors but will appoint no one to replace them. These matters must be decided not from the centre but by the population themselves' (Milyukov, 1921, vol. 1, p. 67). Lvov held both the premiership and the Ministry of the Interior, and his attitude of benevolent anarchy and virtual refusal to set up a central administrative machine permeated government thinking in the early weeks. Local self-government was to be the order of the day until a Constituent Assembly was elected which would reflect democratic opinion and determine the future structure of Russia. The franchise was to be universal (including women), equal and direct, and voting secret. Complete civil rights were granted – freedom of speech, association and religion. As Lenin said, it was the most free government in Europe, possibly the most free ever in a state at war.

Meanwhile, until the Constituent Assembly met, no fundamental decisions could be taken – and yet the Assembly was delayed throughout the year, finally being elected in November. The official reason was that the conditions of war made its election impossible. In the sense that this was true, the government was caught in a vicious circle. No real reform was possible until the Constituent Assembly expressed the will of the people (after all, the Provisional Government was provisional until its convocation), but the Kadets felt increasingly that a truly democratic assembly could not, or should not, be called until after the war was over. Information about local conditions and the electorate had to be gathered. But there was also, as the summer wore on, the undeniable fact that a freely elected assembly would not return a Kadet majority. The liberals did not have a popular base, and indeed had few active members outside Petrograd and Moscow. The peasantry, as had been shown in France in 1848, would decide the issue in an election by weight of numbers, and in Russia they would, and did, vote SR. The leaders of the Soviet might see liberalism as a necessary transitional phase, but the workers and peasants would vote socialist. The liberals faced the classic liberal dilemma of being freely and democratically elected out of office.

Not surprisingly, Kadet enthusiasm for the Constituent Assembly waned and elections were postponed. Meanwhile the country had to be governed, and the government's attempts at local government reorganization, coming on top of local initiatives, led to a proliferation of interlocking and overlapping committees at all levels. The inevitable conflicts produced tension between the centre and the localities, which was to be one of the themes of the revolution and led to lack of confidence in the Provisional

Government by the early summer. Although Prince Lvov had encouraged local initiative, he saw the *zemstvo* as the pivot of local government. New commissars replaced the old tsarist governors, and these were frequently the chairmen of the local *zemstvo* boards, often large landowners, and seen by the peasants as merely a continuation of the old order. *Zemstvos* were to be extended into rural areas at the lowest level of local government – the *volost* (group of villages) – as well as the existing district and provincial organizations. Elections to them at all levels were to be by universal suffrage, and plans were laid for elections at the new *volost* level as an experience in democracy which would also gather electoral rolls needed for the Constituent Assembly. *Volost zemstvos* were then to replace existing peasant *volost* committees. The elections, held from August, were a disaster for the government. The *zemstvo* had never been popular in the villages, and interest in the elections was extremely low. Peasants in practice ignored them and established their own, purely peasant, committees alongside.

Even before the elections to the *volost zemstvos* the writing had been on the wall. By June the elections, again for the first time by universal suffrage, to the local town *dumas* showed that Kadet support in Petrograd and Moscow was only 16 and 21 per cent of the popular vote. The moderate socialists, especially the SRs, won easily, but the Bolsheviks to the alarm of the government, also did well. Milyukov drew the conclusion that the Constituent Assembly should be delayed at least until after the war, the soldiers being blamed for the Bolshevik vote, although he never quite lost the illusion that with time and education the population would see sense and vote liberal. By the time the results of the election for the Constituent Assembly were known in November, he was arguing that the political immaturity of the Russian population made it an unrealizable goal. Earlier Kerensky also referred to there being 'too much ignorance and too little experience among the free people' (Schapiro, 1984, p. 63). Although their support in Petrograd and Moscow had risen by October, the Kadets had only seventeen seats when the Constituent Assembly actually met in January.

Why had the consensus of February evaporated? Because it used existing institutions and concentrated on legal and constitutional reforms, the government was increasingly labelled bourgeois and counter-revolutionary. As the economic situation worsened and social reform was delayed until the Constituent Assembly met, Russia was polarized along class lines. The Kadets believed that they were a national government, not a class one, ruling in the interests of the country as a whole, bringing freedom for all. They argued that they were above party and above class, and hoped to reconcile class antagonisms within a capitalist system and thus make socialism unnecessary. Konovalov worked closely with Menshevik leaders in the Soviet in the first weeks to try to bring this about – by bringing justice to the working man, as he put it. It was partly his labour programme which enabled 'dual power' to work as well as it did in the first few months. On 10 March the Petrograd Society of Industrialists negotiated an agreement with the Soviet which gave the right to strike, freedom for trade unions, an eight-hour day and recognition of factory committees. The number of strikes duly declined for a time as workers' demands for wage increases were met.

It was, however, the issue of the war which was to prove the central problem of the year and which is crucial to any understanding of the failure of the Provisional Government. The Duma leaders, before the February revolution, had opposed the tsarist government not for fighting the war but for conducting it badly. As Foreign Minister, Milyukov was committed to Russia's continuing the war effort as a democratic ally of Britain and France and to fulfilling Russia's obligations under the treaty of 1915. This implied that once the war was won Russia could expect to gain Constantinople and the Straits and possibly Austrian Galicia. Being liberal in 1917 could still mean being imperialist, and Milyukov had always been something of a Pan-Slav. It was over the question of possible territorial gains, clarified by Milyukov in his Note to the Allies on 18 April, that conflict arose with the Petrograd Soviet. Two days later the Soviet leaders organized a demonstration in the capital against the government, the first since February. The crowds called for Milyukov's resignation and rejected any policy of annexation. Shots were fired, casualties resulted, and Milyukov and Guchkov resigned from the government. The honeymoon phase of the revolution was over.

The resulting cabinet crisis was finally resolved on 5 May, when the leaders of the Petrograd Soviet abandoned their previous policy and joined the government, which thus became a liberal-socialist coalition. Five ministers of a total of fifteen were now socialists. The most important were the prominent Mensheviks, I. G. Tsereteli and M. I. Skobelev, and the leader of the SRs, V. M. Chernov. The left wing of the Provisional Government should have been strengthened as a result, but in fact this did not happen. If the radicals among the Kadets, in alliance with the moderate socialists, who had overwhelming electoral support in the summer, had managed to implement land reform and further social change, the fate of Russia might have been different. However, the Mensheviks and SRs were to get the worst of both worlds; branded as lackeys of the bourgeoisie, they shared the Kadets' growing unpopularity as economic conditions deteriorated and the government's policies became more conservative.

Like everybody else, the moderate socialists were divided among themselves. Y. O. Martov and his Menshevik Internationalists were close to Lenin in their views on the war and their belief that power should go to the soviets, while Tsereteli supported the coalition with the Kadets and what he referred to as 'the unity of the national will' (Roobol, 1976, p. 177–8). Chernov and the right wing of the SRs also supported this and urged the primacy of the Constituent Assembly, while its left wing, who were to collaborate with the Bolsheviks by October, supported a peasant revolution. So the Soviet was divided, not only in its detailed programmes for an eventual socialist Russia, but also over whether the revolution should be seen in national or class terms and on the speed at which a transition to socialism could take place. The right wings of the moderate socialist parties agreed with the Kadets in regarding the revolution as a bourgeois one, bringing freedom for everyone in the empire. For them, socialism should be a future goal, not a present reality. Their left wings believed, as Lenin did, that a socialist revolution was an imminent possibility, and regarded the bourgeoisie as enemies of the workers and peasants; as such, they were to be excluded from the future socialist society which would be based on the soviets. The realities of power after May were to highlight the divisions both within the Soviet and between the liberal and socialist wings of the coalition government.

The major problems facing that government in May 1917 were the war, land reform, national minority demands and the growing popular unrest. The Soviet leaders had joined the cabinet at a time of crisis caused by the war, and they regarded this problem as their first priority. Tsereteli, now Minister of the Interior, put forward what he called a policy of 'revolutionary defensism', which rejected any war of aggression and all annexations but accepted the need to fight to defend Russia's borders. He hoped to arrange an international socialist conference in Stockholm which would negotiate a general socialist peace without annexations and impose it on the belligerent imperialist powers. It is a testament to the naïvety of the moderate socialists that they seem to have believed that this was possible. The period from May to July, when they should have been pressing social reform on the Kadets, was spent in a fruitless search for peace. By June, with the army demoralized and disintegrating, Kerensky revised the policy and launched an offensive in Galicia. Its failure, and the subsequent German advance into the Ukraine, sparked off a Ukrainian crisis over local autonomy and the collapse of the first coalition government.

The second coalition, formed in the aftermath of the July Days (see chapter 2), was headed by Kerensky and increased the number of socialists in the cabinet. Government policies, however, moved to the right under pressure of popular discontent and military defeat. The Ukrainian problem was only one of a series of crises over the national minorities and the problem of local self-determination and federalism as against central power, positions taken up by the socialists and the Kadets respectively. By the end of the year, either through military defeat or through local nationalist or separatist movements, many of the national minority areas of the old empire had, for all practical purposes, assumed control of their own destiny. Finland and the Baltic states were to achieve full independence. The Ukraine was largely under German occupation but was also at loggerheads with Petrograd over its demand for autonomy. The Caucasus and areas of central Asia declared themselves autonomous republics in advance of the presumed federalist stance of the Constituent Assembly and preserved their independence during the civil war. By September, even in Russia itself, individual towns were setting up 'republics', as they had done in 1905, ignoring Petrograd and running themselves.

By late summer it was clear that power was slipping away from the central authorities. This was seen in towns like Kronstadt, Tsaritsyn and Baku, but, as the workers' movement and the peasant revolt indicated (see chapter 2), it was not confined to a few areas. Skobelev, as Minister of Labour, supported the workers' demand for wages to be raised in line with inflation and advocated state control of industry, but he failed to prevent the Provisional Government's giving priority to restoring the economy by allaying the fears of the industrialists. Chernov, as Minister of Agriculture, urged the need for immediate land reform on the cabinet, but to no effect. Government policy still decreed that this would be a task for the Constituent Assembly. The creation of land committees to collect data for reform was promised, but these were not established until June. Meanwhile peasant unrest had started. This was particularly serious for the government, since it affected the war effort by encouraging desertion from the army. It was difficult, and by the end of the summer almost impossible, to use the army to suppress the peasant revolt.

The peasantry also increased urban radicalism by disrupting the supply of grain to the towns. As the tsar had done, the Provisional Government tried to control grain supplies. At the end of March a state monopoly in grain was established. Grain was requisitioned at fixed prices, but prices of manufactured goods were not controlled, and hoarding began in the villages. This was not a new problem; the euphoria of February had staved off a crisis earlier in the year. By late summer the situation was again critical. In August the government increased the prices paid to the peasants for their grain by 100 per cent, and merely created rapid inflation. Many rural areas as well as towns bought grain, and by September peasants were preventing grain transports from reaching the urban areas. By that month less than half of Petrograd's requirements reached the city. For the first time in modern Russian history the bulk of the harvest stayed in the countryside. In the capital grain prices doubled between February and June and rose again sharply in the autumn. The harvest on the Volga failed, and transport was not available to move grain from other areas. Severe food shortages were reported from a large number of provincial towns.

Government actions to remedy this situation were too few and too late. The precarious enthusiasm for a democratic government, which had existed in February, was being replaced by conflict and class warfare. The members of both the Provisional Government and the Petrograd Soviet, as they moved from one smoke-filled committee room to another, were increasingly out of touch with the people they claimed to represent. It fell to Kerensky, now Premier and Minister of War, to try to halt this process. His popularity was undoubted, and he was unrivalled in his ability to sway a crowd, at least until the return of Trotsky in May. Kerensky was a socialist, on the far right of the SR party (a Trudovik). Nevertheless he was concerned above all to keep the Kadets as members of the coalition after July. Like almost all Soviet leaders he was unwilling to contemplate a purely socialist government. The Kadets, however, had now been joined by landowner and industrialist groups and were increasingly seen by the mass of the population as bourgeois and reactionary.

Despite this, Kerensky stuck to the policy of coalition. He was a democrat but he was also a patriot. With the failure of the summer offensive and the disintegration of the army on the one hand and the threat of Bolshevism on the other, it was clear that steps had to be taken if democracy was to be saved. Faced with industrialists bewailing the collapse of the economy and calling for a restoration of law and order, Kerensky, on 18 July, appointed General Kornilov as commander-in-chief of the armed forces. Kornilov was entrusted with continuing the war and preventing the collapse of the army. He was a career soldier, from a humble background and popular with his own men. He was one of the few members of the high command prepared to recognize elected soldiers' committees and to work to some extent with the political commissars attached to the general staff by the government. His own commissar, the SR ex-terrorist Boris Savinkov, became deputy War Minister and acted as intermediary between the general and Kerensky. Kornilov, however, was no politician and had acquired a popular reputation as a reactionary during the April crisis when he had been in charge of the Petrograd garrison.

Kornilov accepted the post with conditions which would restore discipline, conditions which Kerensky was at first prepared to accept. The death penalty for mutiny and insubordination at the front had already been restored by the government before Kornilov's appointment. This was now to be extended to the urban garrisons, political propaganda in the army was to be stopped, and firm action was to be taken against the Bolsheviks. Kerensky was in a difficult position. He was anxious for Kadet support and personally convinced of the need for measures to restore discipline. However, he was also vice-chairman of the Soviet, which would certainly not support such measures, and that could leave him the prisoner of the conservative groups, if not of Kornilov himself. There is no evidence that Kornilov intended to create a personal dictatorship. Nevertheless, as the State Conference in Moscow in August showed, he was the hero of the right, and bodies like the Society for the Economic Rehabilitation of Russia and the Republican Centre did see him as a possible dictator. The British also looked to him as a strong man who could save Russia and keep her in the war.

Kerensky and Kornilov communicated through intermediaries in an atmosphere of increasing suspicion and misinformation. After Riga fell to the Germans on 21 August, Kornilov proposed to march on Petrograd to forestall an expected Bolshevik uprising. He undoubtedly thought that Kerensky had agreed. Kerensky's own role was unclear but dubious. Certainly he panicked, denounced Kornilov as a traitor and dismissed him. Whatever the general's original motives, his decision to proceed was rebellion. He was stopped, but not by Kerensky, whose standing never recovered. He was stopped by the railwaymen who halted the troop trains, by the trade unions, and by a remarkable popular movement of workers-turned-militiamen who moved to protect their revolution. The Soviet galvanized itself into action to organize the movement, but it was the Bolshevik activists, many released from prison where they had been since the July Days, who led the movement and reaped the political credit. The rapid revitalization of the Bolsheviks after their defeat in July was the most momentous result of the *Kornilovshchina*.

The Provisional Government never recovered from the Kornilov episode. A Democratic Conference met on 14 September to decide the future form of government but achieved nothing. A pre-parliament was set up to sit until the Constituent Assembly met, and yet another coalition was established, but when the Bolsheviks seized power in October Russia had no government worthy of the name. The liberals, if not the moderate socialists, drew the conclusion that democracy had failed and turned to the generals. Workers and peasants were also to look to non-parliamentary solutions. The masses had not seen the revolution in February as being primarily about legal and constitutional reform. They had looked to it to bring about radical social change, and it had failed to do so. As land was not given and the economic situation in the towns worsened, the mass movement became more violent and more radical. By October power was to go to the party most identified with that mass radicalism.

2 The Rise of the Bolsheviks, April–October 1917

The main conflict in 1917 was less between the Provisional Government and the Petrograd Soviet than between the intellectuals of both bodies and the workers, peasants and soldiers. It was by keeping the Bolshevik party separate from the liberal-socialist coalition and by identifying it with the demands of the popular movement that Lenin was to come to power.

Lenin's rejection of the moderate position adopted by the Bolshevik Central Committee in March, and his siding with the radical activists in the lower ranks of the party, was first made manifest in his *Letters from Afar* and spelled out in the *April Theses* on his return to Russia. His proposals were initially rejected by the Central Committee by 13 votes to 2. The left-wing Menshevik chronicler of the revolution, N. N. Sukhanov, has testified to the shock that Lenin's approach caused the party apparatus. 'I shall never forget that thunder-like speech', he wrote later, 'which startled and amazed not only me, a heretic who had accidentally dropped in, but all the believers. I am certain that no-one had expected anything of the sort' (Sukhanov, 1955, p. 280). Not only did it identify party policy with the left wing Bolshevik militants; it also identified it with mass radicalism, an adoption of popular spontaneity, in contrast to the Lenin of 1902 and *What is to be Done?*, but a return in many ways to Bolshevik actions in 1905.

During the earlier revolution the Bolshevik party had actively encouraged working-class membership and had adopted a radical stance, calling for an armed uprising against the regime.

Lenin's views, however, now went much further than they had done in 1905. He now declared that the Provisional Government was not to be supported and that the revolution could begin to move to a socialist phase. Lenin's analysis of the situation in April was radically different from that of the moderate socialist leaders of the Petrograd Soviet and the moderates on his own Central Committee. It was not a matter of conditional support for the Provisional Government or even of a Constituent Assembly or a parliamentary republic. For Lenin, the bourgeois stage of the revolution was over, and parliamentary institutions were no longer appropriate, although this did not stop the Bolsheviks campaigning for the convening of the Constituent Assembly. The bourgeoisie was too weak and the organs of the proletariat were too advanced for any progressive bourgeois phase of the revolution to be developed. Moreover, the Provisional Government's commitment to the Allies and the war effort would tie its fate to the common collapse of the capitalist-imperialist states that the war, in Lenin's eyes, would bring. Thus, he argued, the Provisional Government was bound to become counter-revolutionary, and indeed was already doing so. The only way forward for the revolution was through a government of the soviets, once Bolshevik control of these bodies was assured.

The programme put forward by the Bolshevik leader in the *April Theses* was thus clear and uncompromising: no support for the government, the war or the policy of revolutionary defensism; a call for the transfer of power to the soviets; nationalization of land and banking; and the abolition of the police force, the army and the bureaucracy. The revolution was already in transition to its second stage of placing power in the hands of the proletariat and the poor peasantry. The soviets must first bring production

27

and distribution of goods under their control and then start to build socialism. The bewildered Central Committee finally agreed to this programme, partly because, for many of them, the 'transition' to the second stage could take a long period of time. On 14 April, just under two weeks after the *April Theses* were delivered, a conference of the Bolshevik organizations in Petrograd accepted Lenin's views by 37 votes to 3, and the Central Committee reluctantly agreed to implement the programme. Meanwhile the tasks of the party were clear: to strengthen the soviets from below and increase Bolshevik influence over them; to radicalize their policies and build up workers' militias; to win over peasants and soldiers; and at every opportunity to expose the reactionary nature of the Kadets and their Menshevik and SR allies. Lenin's tasks over the next six months were to gain popular support and to convert his party to the idea of a takeover of power. In many ways the first task was to prove easier than the second. Frequently, for example in July, the party leadership followed, or was swept along by, the mass movement which, as Lenin admitted, was more militant and left wing than the party. The various strata of the party leadership remained, as in February, disunited over policy and methods. Nevertheless the support from the working class and the army units nearest to the capital showed a steady rise. This can be plotted for Petrograd by the election returns for the city *duma* in May and August and the Constituent Assembly in November. From May to November, in Petrograd, the Bolshevik share of the vote rose from 20.4 to 45 per cent, with support for the moderate socialists showing a significant fall from 56 to 19 per cent.

As the Bolsheviks' popularity rose, so did party membership. In the process the party was to change out of all recognition. By October it was a mass party, not the elite intellectual grouping of 1903 or of popular imagination. Figures for membership are difficult to establish, but it would seem that the party grew tenfold in the course of the year to rather more than a quarter of a million. The vast majority of members by October were workers and had joined the party since February. At the Sixth Party Congress in July, 94 per cent of the delegates had become Bolsheviks since 1914. Again in contrast to popular belief, they were not highly organized or united, although they had probably more cohesion and certainly stronger leadership than their rivals. But there were great differences in approach between the Central Committee, local 'sub-elites' in district committees and soviets, and 'sub-sub-elites' in the factories. Local activists, like their supporters, tended to act with remarkable independence. The party slogans – 'Peace, Bread, Land' and 'All Power to the Soviets' – the party press and agitators identified the Bolsheviks as the party of soviet power: the only party which could achieve such power, safeguard the gains of February against a rightward-turning Provisional Government and act in the interests of the masses.

The nature and aspirations of the urban movement in 1917 have been the subject of much recent scholarship and even more acrimonious debate. Anarchist historiography from 1918 onwards has argued that Lenin took over and betrayed a popular movement that was essentially anarchist and syndicalist in inspiration (see Glossary). Before considering how far ideologies of any kind motivated the movement, it is useful to examine the Russian working class in some detail, since it was in many ways different from its western counterparts. The proletariat's ties with the village remained far stronger than in western Europe, especially in Moscow and provincial towns although, by 1914, less so in St Petersburg. At the end of the nineteenth century most urban workers were single men, who left their families in the countryside, still owned a little land and returned regularly to their villages. Thus an urban proletarian consciousness was slow to develop. Indeed, it can be said that peasant radicalism penetrated the cities as much as urban ideas influenced the villages. Workers' models came from the countryside. The *starostas* or elders, recognized by the government in 1903 as factory representatives, stemmed from the heads of village communes; the *zemlyachestvo* was an informal grouping of workers from the same village or region established in the towns for mutual support, and, as the Vyborg Bolsheviks showed, it could lead to political organizations.

St Petersburg was exceptional in the Russian empire for its more westernized and settled proletariat, for the highly advanced nature of its industry and the enormous size of many of its factories. By 1914, 70 per cent of all enterprises in the capital employed over 1,000 people, and state-run metallurgical works could be many times that size. The Putilov factory employed 30,000 men and was divided into forty-one shops. Historians now stress the importance of shop identification or craft consciousness to the worker in an environment where trade unions were weak or illegal. Trade unions, of course, flourished in 1917, with three million members by October, but many workers still identified more readily with their trade or their factory. It is important to remember that the workforce differed greatly even within the same factory. Worker memoirs stress the differences between skilled and unskilled labour; between 'hot' shops like foundries in the big metallurgical plants, and 'cold' craft shops for skilled work; between new and older established workers. A literate, politically conscious, skilled craftsman would look down on recent peasant arrivals. It was these unskilled, new workers who participated in the spontaneous bouts of disorder in the early days of the revolution, when factory managers and owners were beaten or 'carted out' – put in a wheelbarrow and tipped into the street or a local river. Such acts were often denounced by their more organized colleagues.

The problem of the relationship between spontaneity and organization, between economic and political motivation, is a difficult one. Demands for economic change could mean calls for political change as the only way such demands could be met. Unorganized groups like women workers formed their own organizations in 1917, and extreme

30

radicalism could be, and often was, associated with a low level of political consciousness. Moreover, the experience of 1905, and more recently of the war, had helped to radicalize opinion generally. Of the new workers, women on the whole played a passive role after February, and labour leaders were reluctant to allow separate women's sections. The young were more active, joining parties with a reputation for action: the Bolsheviks and the anarchists. One estimate is that nearly 20 per cent of those who joined the Bolshevik party in 1917 were under twenty-one and 28 per cent of Red Guards were under that age.

Political consciousness meant different things to different people. To many ordinary workers it meant hatred of the war, the monarchy and the bourgeoisie, and an identification with the organs of direct street-level democracy of the revolutionary year: local soviets and factory committees. It might not mean, at least in the first half of 1917, party consciousness in the sense of differentiating among party programmes. As late as September in Moscow it was possible to be asked if 'a Bolshevik' stood for 'a large man' (Koenker, 1981, p. 187). Individual charisma or oratory by a particular party activist could sway whole factories to support a particular party. In the capital, where literacy rates were higher, there was probably more awareness, and the experience of constant participation in the events of 1917 itself increased it. Workers joined factory committees, trade unions and soviets, and voted in elections for them and for town *dumas* and, finally, for the Constituent Assembly. Initially it would appear that party allegiances were not necessarily seen as important and might even be opposed as dividing the workers' movement. Institutions like soviets or factory committees, except at the top of the institutional hierarchy, like the Petrograd Soviet, did not at first operate along party lines. In the early days of the revolution in Moscow parties were explicitly excluded from such bodies as the Bureau of Trade Unions, and soviets outside the capital were often non-party, or at least inter-party. Several towns formed united Social Democratic

31

organizations in an attempt to reunite Bolsheviks and Mensheviks. The head of the Soviet of Workers' Deputies in Kronstadt was non-party for some months. However, once a worker was elected as a representative, he had increasingly to acquire a party affiliation, and as the year wore on elections of all sorts were overwhelmingly on party platforms.

The most politicized section of the labour force of the capital was undoubtedly the skilled craftsmen of the metallurgical industries. If one force behind February had been the radicalized new workers hit by rising prices and food shortages, the other was the skilled elite of master craftsmen who had grievances of their own. Their traditional privileged status had been whittled away during the war under the impact of prices rising faster than wages, which reduced their differentials, and mass-production techniques, which removed part of the need for craft skills. They were to emerge as leaders of the factory committees which in February quickly and spontaneously formed from the factories themselves. The movement was strongest in the state-owned factories where the managers often fled or were ousted in the first few days. Most of these were armaments works, and thus the factory committees which were formed to keep the factories running were at first in favour of 'revolutionary defensism' and were not anxious to abandon the war effort. Initial party influence was often from the SRs, and they supported the policies of the Petrograd Soviet. But if Bolshevik representation was at first small it was to grow rapidly. By the first conference of Petrograd factory committees in May the Bolsheviks were in a majority, and the movement was the first forum that they were to secure in their revolutionary advance.

In 1917 it was the factory committees which represented workers' interests. An eight-hour day, wage increases of between 30 and 50 per cent, and the acceptance of workers' committees to supervise management were among their early achievements. They organized factory militias to protect factory property and impose revolutionary order, and these quickly came into conflict with the all-class civil militias formed by the Provisional Government to replace the old police force. By July there were also 10,000 more radicalized Red Guards in the capital – a number which was to double after the Kornilov affair – and the Bolsheviks were to benefit from their control of these armed detachments by the autumn. Factory committees also tried, not always with success, to keep labour discipline and to punish lateness and drunkenness at work. They ran cultural activities, organized food supplies and arbitrated in disputes over hiring and firing labour. As the trade unions got organized, some of these duties were taken over by them, but it was the factory committees which mattered most to the ordinary worker in 1917.

It is on the activities of the committees that the vexed question of workers' control and anarchist influence centres. It is clear that in February they were seen as organs to co-operate with and to supervise management, and not as a radical left-wing experiment. They had their roots in the 1905 revolution and the *starosta* system. The Provisional Government legalized them in April. Control was interpreted in the Russian sense of the word *kontrol* as meaning supervision, not self-management. Nevertheless by the summer any possibility of co-operation between management and labour seemed to be at an end. Large industrialists, taking advantage of the right turn in government policy after July, tried to re-establish control over their factories. In the south of Russia especially this led to several armed clashes, and some establishments were taken over by their workers. Meanwhile 568 factories in Petrograd closed between February and July with the loss of over 100,000 jobs, and the number of strikes rocketed. According to government figures, 40,000 people were unemployed in the capital by the autumn.

The large wage increases of the early weeks were soon nullified by increasing prices and food shortages, leading to queues and discontent. By October the bread ration was almost half what it had been in February. The polarization between the 'haves' and the 'have-nots' of Russian society led to a heightening of class conflict and was clearly reflected in election results in Petrograd and Moscow. Much of the Bolshevik appeal lay in articulating these antagonisms. Meanwhile factory committees reacted to the situation by intervening more directly in factory management, and in a few cases by taking over their factories and running them themselves. S. A. Smith (1983) has argued convincingly that this was a reaction to economic crisis and the threat of redundancy, and was not motivated by any anarchist or syndicalist belief in profit-sharing or workers' management. The workers' aim was to keep their jobs and stave off 'Tsar Hunger'. Anarchists were active in the movement and indeed co-operated closely with the Bolsheviks. But there were never more than about 8 per cent of anarchist delegates elected to the factory committees' central bodies, and it was Bolshevik, not anarchist, slogans that were adopted. Some factory committees did show talent for management. In some cases envoys were sent to the countryside in search of fuel and raw materials. The factory committees had a touching faith that the economy could be righted if owner 'sabotage' could be ended and the workers were in overall control.

Moreover, the anarchist rejection of all central state power was not widespread. Factory committees believed in local, decentralized initiative, but they produced their own centralizing bureaucracy, and an All-Russian Conference of Factory Committees met in October. Leading figures in the movement were members of the Bolshevik party and saw nothing contradictory in that. Lenin himself in 1917 also seemed to regard workers' control of factories (in the supervisory sense that he understood the term) and state control of the overall economy as quite compatible. The question was: what sort of state? Before 1918 both Bolsheviks and the factory committee movement seemed to believe that workers' control of production at a grassroots level was quite compatible with an overall control of the economy by a workers' state.

It was significant that the Bolsheviks had greatest appeal to the organizations closest to the masses and most involved in the street-level direct democracy of the revolutionary year. As the soviet network became more centralized and hierarchical, with its own bureaucracy of paid officials and executive committees who increasingly took decisions in committee rooms away from the mass plenary sessions, popular confidence became centred in factory committees and the lowest tier of the soviet hierarchy, and it was here that the Bolsheviks, and other left-wing extremists who allied with them, gained support. One historian has described the Bolsheviks in 1917 as a 'catch-all party of the radical left' (Service, 1979, p. 49). Anarchists, Menshevik Internationalists, Left SRs and Trotsky's Interdistrict Group supported and merged with Lenin's party over the summer and autumn. The popularity of the slogan 'All Power to the Soviets' had little to do with the Petrograd Soviet as such by the summer. After the July Days Lenin temporarily replaced the slogan by 'All Power to the Factory Committees', but this was reversed when it became obvious that the appeal of the soviet idea had not diminished. It meant that working people could run their own affairs through hundreds of local town, district and suburban soviets. The extreme example, and one which saw itself as a model for the rest of Russia to follow, was the naval base of Kronstadt.

From the early days of the February revolution Kronstadt was run by its own local soviet of workers and sailors. It refused to acknowledge the sovereignty of the Provisional Government, and 'dual power' never operated there. After May and the formation of the coalition government it also refused to accept the policies of the Petrograd Soviet, and thereafter, although a compromise formula was patched up, for all practical purposes Kronstadt governed itself. Direct elections from units, ships and factories selected delegates to the town soviet who were directly accountable and could be instantly recalled. The soviet was run not by intellectuals but by the skilled workers needed to man a modern naval base, and visitors contrasted its lively meetings with the sleepier debates of the capital. Mass meetings in Anchor Square heard the great names of the revolution, and all left-wing parties were represented on the soviet, though none predominated. The Bolsheviks had about a third of the seats by the summer; SR Maximalists (see Glossary) were perhaps the most influential group, and anarchists again were under-represented on committees, although influential. Many delegates were deliberately non-party, but Kronstadt supported Bolshevik policies in July and again in October, regarding the Bolsheviks as the only party which 'meant business'.

As a self-running workers' community, egalitarian (although restricted to men), and interpreting the revolution in terms of social transformation, Kronstadt had a vision of the future which was in many ways the nearest the revolution produced to the anarchist ideal of a toilers' republic, a federation of self-governing local soviets and communes. Nevertheless, as I. Getzler (1983) has shown, even in this case some form of centralized soviet government was envisaged. Other towns produced somewhat similar 'republics' in 1917, but Kronstadt was by far the best example of soviet power in action and was also the most influential. Since Kronstadt was only just down river from Petrograd, the sailors could, and did, march into the capital and influence events there. This was best manifested in the July Days.

The July Days brought together the discontents of workers, soldiers and sailors in an explosive demonstration of popular dissatisfaction against the coalition government. The demonstrations started in June in response to the army's growing discontent with the failure to end the war. Order No. 1 had in one swoop overturned the old order in the army. The new soldiers' committees were at first mainly run by 'intellectuals in uniform', often educated Jews barred from holding commissions in the tsarist army, who were serving as doctors or engineers. Many were Mensheviks and supported the Petrograd Soviet and the policy of 'revolutionary defensism'. By the end of April the patriotic appeals of the Provisional Government were no longer being listened to. Although the front line held, desertion rates increased, and lynchings of officers were reported. Defeatist and pacifist attitudes among the troops led to widespread fraternization with the enemy. The soldiers' committees became more radical, and by May Bolshevik propaganda was seen by increasing numbers of the soldiers as best articulating what they considered to be important. As A. Wildman has said, the Bolsheviks became 'the chief conduit of rebellion against the military order and against the resumption of active operations' (1980, p. 372).

The mutinous Petrograd garrison had not been dispersed after February, and, although its initial allegiance had been to the Petrograd Soviet, by the summer the Bolsheviks were winning the battle in which all parties were engaged for its support. In response to pressure from garrison troops, the Bolshevik Military Organization proposed an anti-war demonstration for 10 June. Lenin supported them, but the Central Committee was hesitant. The Military Organization, however, had put great effort into gaining influence over the troops and was loath to risk losing it. Nevertheless, after a prohibition by the Petrograd Soviet of all demonstrations, the plan was abandoned. The Soviet itself then sanctioned a demonstration for 18 June, the day Kerensky's summer offensive in Galicia started, only to watch with dismay as the march amply proved the extent of the Bolsheviks' following. Eyewitnesses described the scene as a sea of Bolshevik flags and banners with slogans calling for 'All Power to the Soviets' and 'Down with the Ten Capitalist Ministers'.

The next test of public opinion came over the government's decision to move some regiments out of the capital to participate in the war offensive. The first machine-gun regiment, heavily influenced by both the Bolsheviks and the anarchists, resisted the call and arranged a mass demonstration for 3 July, calling on Kronstadt for aid.

The Bolshevik Central Committee again ordered non-participation, and the Military Organization again ignored them. In Kronstadt F. F. Raskolnikov, the Bolshevik leader, persuaded the sailors that Petrograd was already in revolt and that an insurrection was possible. As the coalition government collapsed over the Ukrainian crisis in the aftermath of the German advance, the crowds again came on to the streets, and the Kronstadt sailors arrived in the capital for the second time in a month. Lenin, initially reluctant to involve the party, recognized the danger of losing influence to the anarchists and the motley groups of radicals on the party's left. From 4 July the Bolsheviks led the movement. In many ways the July Days were a disaster for the party. An armed and sullen crowd, unclear about its aim and easily panicked into firing its rifles, converged on the Tauride Palace calling for the Soviet to take power. It quickly became clear that the Soviet would do no such thing, and neither the crowd nor their Bolshevik leaders were in a position to do it for them. One workman called to Chernov, 'take power, you son of a bitch, when it's offered to you' (Milyukov, 1921, vol. 1, p. 244), and the unfortunate Chernov had to be rescued from the enraged mob by Trotsky.

By 5 July troops loyal to the Soviet were in control. The Kronstadters retreated demoralized and discredited and none too pleased with their Bolshevik leadership. The Bolsheviks themselves were attacked and arrested, their presses destroyed and accusations of being German agents levelled at them, to some effect. Lenin fled to Finland, and the party's Sixth Congress was held under almost pre-revolutionary conspiratorial conditions. But party membership did not fall significantly, and the Bolsheviks were to recover their standing with remarkable swiftness, helped by Kerensky's growing unpopularity and the Kornilov affair. Soviet power, rather than party programmes or the Constituent Assembly, was seen by the masses as the solution to their problems, and only the Bolsheviks were really identified with soviet power. Menshevik support collapsed in the main towns. By 9 September the Bolsheviks had a majority in the Petrograd Soviet with Trotsky as chairman, followed shortly by Moscow, and Kronstadt and the northern fronts supported them. The party was now in a position to ride the popular wave into power. The last factor in the Bolshevik support was the peasantry.

The SR leader, Chernov, once called the peasantry the 'true autocrat of Russia', and the peasant revolt and its consequences, as well as the peasants' electoral power, were to bear him out in 1917. The impact of Stolypin's land reforms, the growing industrialization, educational reforms and, above all, the First World War had all affected the peasantry since their last revolt in 1905. However, the revolt of 1917 still showed many traditional features. The initial reaction to February in the villages was favourable. Resolutions promising support to the new regime came in from the countryside, deserters from the army were returned, and the revolution was celebrated with festivities and church services. Grain was even supplied to army depots. But if the mood of the peasants was favourable to the Provisional Government it was also expectant. The peasants expected that the land would now be given to them. Their view was that private property should be abolished without compensation and that land, like air or water, should be seen as a natural commodity, free to those who used it. 'The land must belong to those who work it with their hands, to those whose sweat flows' (Gill, 1979, p. 155) was the gist of innumerable peasant resolutions. Everyone, even the local landowner, should retain as much land as could be farmed by his family. This was SR policy, and the traditional SR links with the peasantry remained strong early in the year. Intellectuals in the villages were asked for guidance. However, as the weeks passed, the peasants began to take matters into their own hands. SRs who advised waiting for the Constituent Assembly were ignored. Local landlords found that no force was available to stop peasants grazing cattle, felling trees or stealing property. The peasant reaction tended to be 'it's all the same; it will soon be ours.'

Newspapers were widely read and listened to, the Constituent Assembly was frequently invoked, and the demand for speakers and education was high. But land was all important; it was rare for a peasant to distinguish between projected and established laws, and everything was expected to change immediately. By the time the All-Russian Congress of Peasant Deputies met in May, the revolt was already under way and the villages were running themselves. The congress had a 50 per cent SR membership, but Chernov allowed Lenin to outmanœuvre him at what should have been his natural forum. The number of Bolshevik delegates was tiny and their influence in the villages was almost non-existent. Nevertheless they alone were prepared to call for the immediate granting of all land to the peasantry and to encourage the peasants to take it themselves. The congress agreed in principle that land should be placed under the direction of land committees, and the peasants took this as an invitation to seize it.

Incidents were at first traditional – illegal timber cutting, pasturing stock on private land, refusing to pay rents, demanding high wages and seizing state or chuch land. Stolypin's 'separators', those peasants who had left the village commune after 1906, were forced back into the communal unit, and their land redivided. By June, land belonging to landlords was also being expropriated. After a quiet period in late summer when the harvest was gathered in, the peasant revolt became more widespread and more violent in September. Country houses were destroyed, land and timber were taken under the control of the village on a large scale, and some landlords were killed. Bands of deserters and seizures of government vodka supplies added to the violence. Most affected was a broad belt of land stretching from the Ukraine across the central agricultural region to the Volga.

The peasants were politically conscious in the sense that they blamed the landowners for their plight and were aware that the government, if it wished, had the power to grant them land. Peasants active at *volost* level or involved in peasant committees were often SRs, the only party most peasants knew about. However, at village level what organization there was in the peasant revolt came from the commune itself. The traditional peasant commune re-emerged, from the plethora of committees and soviets, as the strongest force in the countryside in 1917. By September many of the old commune elders were finding themselves replaced by younger men, or by those returning from the army or the towns to claim their share of the land. Many of these were Bolshevik supporters, and the party tried to use them to increase their influence in the villages. The *zemlyachestvos* of Petrograd and Kronstadt alone were connected with twenty provinces and had over 40,000 members. Through these organizations Bolshevik propaganda reached the villages and in many areas was well received. The SR party split in two as its left wing broke away to form the Left SR party and supported the Bolsheviks. Lenin, anyway, had adopted SR terminology, and his land decree in October was to be taken word for word from SR documents. The Bolsheviks had created a rural Red Guard early in the year, and their slogans nicely sum up the mixture of policies: 'Proletarians of All Countries Unite' and 'Long Live Land and Liberty'.

As land was seized by the commune and redivided among families in strips and according to family size in the time-honoured way, a levelling operation took place. The peasantry had finally achieved its old dream of a 'black repartition' – an egalitarian division of all land organized and controlled by the peasants themselves. Lenin's attitude to all this was pragmatic: it could not be stopped, and the Bolsheviks stood to gain from it. What was happening in the countryside was certainly not what Lenin desired. However, he accepted it as a necessary first, or capitalist, phase which would satisfy the petty-bourgeois instincts of the peasantry, by giving them the ownership of the land as private property, and ensure peasant support for a proletarian revolution. No peasant would oppose a government which promised peace and land, even if the wider nature of Bolshevik policies was unknown in the villages. Lenin, at the end of 1917, hoped that the next stage of the revolution would see a class struggle within the peasantry and a poor peasant–proletarian alliance, which would eventually lead to a socialist organization of agriculture.

By early September, in Lenin's eyes all the pieces had come together. He could argue that his analysis of the Provisional Government as becoming counter-revolutionary was proved by the Kornilov affair, the Bolsheviks had a majority in the Petrograd and Moscow soviets, and the mass of the people saw the party as the only available alternative to an increasingly unsatisfactory government. With support from the masses the party could now seize power, and Lenin was fully prepared to do so. On 12 September he wrote from Finland to the Central Committee urging an immediate insurrection. 'History will not forgive us', he wrote, 'if we do not assume power now' (*Collected Works*, hereafter *CW*, 1964, vol. 26, p. 21).

3 The Establishment of Bolshevik Power, 1917–1918

The months following mid-September were months of revolutionary euphoria, constant argument and confusion, as much within the Bolshevik party as outside it. Conflict within the party hierarchy, so noticeable in the early part of the year, increased rather than diminshed in October. On 15 Septembter the Central Committee received two letters from Lenin, who was still in Finland – letters known later as *The Bolsheviks Must Assume Power* and *Marxism and Insurrection*. As in April, the Central Committee was unprepared for Lenin's apparent change of policy. Even the Military Organization and the local Petrograd Bolshevik committee, radical earlier in the year, had been shocked into caution by the aftermath of the July Days. To Lenin, by contrast, any comparison with July was foolish. The situation had changed to the Bolsheviks' advantage. The party now controlled the major soviets, the government was weaker, the peasant revolt had completed the radicalization of the proletariat, and class antagonisms had increased. Sensing that this was the best opportunity the party was ever to have, he urged immediate action. He bombarded the Central Committee with instructions and threats to resign, but nothing was seriously discussed until Lenin returned to the capital, in disguise, on 7 October.

As Trotsky was later to write, without Lenin there would have been no October revolution.

Under pressure, on 10 October the Central Committee agreed in principle to an uprising but set no date. Two of Lenin's closest lieutenants, Kamenev and G. Y. Zinoviev, dissented and publicized their arguments in a letter, which, to Lenin's fury, was leaked to Maxim Gorky's newspaper *Novaya Zhizn* (*New Life*). From that moment it was common knowledge that the Bolsheviks were planning a coup. Almost everyone involved in the October uprising had a different concept of revolution, but within the party three lines of argument may be distinguished. Lenin's was to advocate immediate armed insurrection by the proletariat, led and organized by the Bolsheviks before the forthcoming Second All-Russian Congress of Soviets. Zinoviev and Kamenev advised delay. Afraid of further July Days, they argued that the future of not only the Russian revolution but also the expected European one should not be put in jeopardy by an over-hasty and risky *coup d'état*. The Bolsheviks had support from the proletariat and a significant part of the army but not yet the mass of the population outside the major cities. That support was growing, however, and they urged waiting until the Constituent Assembly elections, or at the very least until after the Congress of Soviets met. The congress could then itself take power with a large Bolshevik majority which in time would draw the masses to its support. This would give a degree of legality to the proceedings and avoid violence.

The implications of this position were important. An assumption of power by the Congress of Soviets, even with a Bolshevik majority, would mean a coalition socialist government, which Lenin was determined to avoid — particularly a coalition with the Mensheviks. He saw the revolution as introducing the Marxist stage of a dictatorship of the proletariat, in which, as capitalism is finally overthrown, the proletariat seizes power and uses state means of repression to eliminate its enemies, the bourgeoisie. Only after this transitional stage has been completed can a perfect socialist society be built. For Lenin, the revolution was to be a transfer of power specifically to the working class – a revolution for and by the proletariat supported by the poor peasants, not a revolution for the benefit of all classes. He therefore argued that the proletariat should be led by its vanguard party (the Bolsheviks) alone. He was not concerned with the revolution's legitimacy or what he scornfully called 'formal' majorities. 'No revolution', he wrote, 'ever waits for that' (*CW*, 1964, vol. 26, p. 21). Support was present where it mattered, theoretically and in practice, and could not wait on peasant votes. Since July he had been committed to what Marx had called 'insurrection as an art'. The timing for Lenin was vital. A party seizure of power at the head of an armed uprising would be sanctioned by the Congress of Soviets after it had happened.

The third position was Trotsky's. After over a decade of bitter hostility to Lenin and to his concept of the vanguard party, Trotsky had finally joined the Bolsheviks in August. His conversion was the result of a number of factors: a recognition after 1905 that some party organization was necessary, the wide and relatively democratic nature of the Bolshevik party in 1917, and the policies adopted by Lenin since his return to Russia. The *April Theses* were near enough to Trotsky's theory of permanent revolution for him to feel that Lenin had adopted his own position. To Lenin, Trotsky was a valuable ally. It was Trotsky who was the tribune of the year, keeping a high public profile, and whose oratory could sway crowds. Since he had regained his old 1905 ascendancy over the Petrograd Soviet and become chairman, Trotsky was in a position to organize the revolution itself. Trotsky's own view of the situation is not easy to establish, but his tactic, and the one that was ultimately to be used, was to synchronize the uprising with the opening of the congress and thus legitimize the takeover under the cover of the Soviet. Trotsky later described this as a brilliant policy, but it was his, not Lenin's. Lenin, although appreciative of Trotsky's organizational skill, was anxious to act as quickly as possible. The force behind the uprising also came from Trotsky's control of the Military Revolutionary Committee (MRC), which had been formed by the Soviet early in October against expected government repression.

Party activists had warned that an uprising in the name of the party would get only limited support. A call for 'All Power to the Soviets' would be more popular, but there was much evidence of lack of faith in party solutions in the factories and on the streets by October. Even an appeal couched in terms of the Soviet would not guarantee widespread response on the eve of the forthcoming congress. In the end, as Victor Serge later wrote, 'the whole offensive was conducted under the formal pretext of defence' (Serge, 1972, p. 68). Kerensky gave Trotsky the ideal solution by making it possible for him to claim that the soviets were under threat from government repression, and this is what guaranteed support. Amid rumours that Petrograd was to be evacuated and surrendered to the Germans, the Military Revolutionary Committee took over the garrison from its commander and thus effectively gained control of the city a good week before the uprising on the 24th. Kerensky initiated criminal proceedings, closed two Bolshevik newspapers and announced that he intended to act against the party. Using the MRC (the Red Guards were relatively unimportant), Trotsky took the key points of the city on the night of 24–5 October and the Kronstadt sailors, arriving in the morning, completed the job. The initial proclamation announcing the fall of the Provisional Government issued at 10 a.m. declared that power was in the hands of the MRC. By the time the Congress of Soviets assembled that evening only the Winter Palace was still holding out, the remnants of the Provisional Government guarded by a women's battalion and an officer cadet corps. In striking contrast to February, and to later film portrayals, this was not a mass uprising. Relatively few people were actively involved. If it were a coup – and Lenin denied this, calling it an armed uprising of the urban masses – it was one enthusiastically suported by the proletariat and accepted by the peasantry. In the capital, although not in Moscow and some other towns, it was remarkably bloodless. Kerensky had fled to raise Cossack support, and General Krasnov, the Cossack leader and tsarist general, reached the outskirts of the city before being stopped and then released by his captors.

Although the insurrection was in the name of the Soviet, neither the Petrograd Soviet nor the assembling Congress was involved. Right-wing SRs and Mensheviks walked out of the congress as a protest, thus earning their place in Trotsky's 'dustbin of history' and, more importantly, forfeiting any hope of influencing the situation. Only Left SRs and other left-wing splinter groups remained to join the Bolshevik majority in listening to Lenin's declaration of intent. 'We shall now proceed to build, on the space cleared of historical rubbish, the airy, towering edifice of socialist society' (*CW*, 1964, vol. 26, p. 80).

Soviet power was proclaimed to great enthusiasm, but it was far from clear what this meant. Trotsky had managed to merge the ideas of Bolshevik power and 'All Power to the Soviets', yet where did power lie on 26 October? Within the party leadership at first all sides seem to have believed that their view had prevailed. Lenin had, if only just, got his way, and a Bolshevik-led insurrection had been sanctioned by the Soviet. Kamenev, however, accepted the chairmanship of the congress and Zinoviev became editor of the Soviet newspaper *Izvestiya* on the assumption that power would pass to the Soviet's Executive Committee. The Soviet did, in fact, have an administration capable of becoming a government. However, to everyone's surprise Lenin announced the creation of a new body, the Council of People's Commissars (Sovnarkom). Although this was a purely Bolshevik body (the Left SRs initially refusing to be involved), it was not the Bolshevik Central Committee, and the relationship between the Central Executive Committee of the Soviet (CEC), Sovnarkom and the Central Committee of the party was unclear – and was not helped by the fact that many of the same people sat on all three bodies.

At once the question of a coalition socialist government came to the top of the political agenda. Zinoviev and Kamenev started negotiations with the Menshevik and SR leadership who, having withdrawn from the congress, had established a rival body, the Committee for the Salvation of the Fatherland and the Revolution. The possibility of a government which excluded both Lenin and Trotsky was seriously discussed. The Bolshevik leader demanded that his lieutenants submit to party discipline, but it was not until 4 November that the possibility of an all-socialist regime was finally abandoned. At a stormy meeting of the Soviet's Executive Committee, which expressed disquiet at a range of Bolshevik policies, the Bolshevik moderates read out a statement: 'It is vital to form a socialist government from all parties [represented] in the Soviets. ... We consider that a purely Bolshevik government has no choice but to maintain itself by political terror. ... We cannot follow this course' (Keep, 1979, p. 77). Four People's Commissars, apart from Zinoviev and Kamenev, and six other government officials resigned. The Petrograd Bolshevik leader Shlyapnikov and A. V. Lunacharsky, newly appointed as Commissar of Enlightenment, expressed sympathy with their position. Zinoviev, Kamenev and three others also resigned from the Central Committee of the party. Thus within two weeks of taking power the party had split radically. Party discipline was to reassert itself, however. Within days Zinoviev had recanted: 'We prefer to make mistakes with millions of workers and soldiers and to die together with them rather than to step to one side at this decisive, historic moment' (Bone, 1974, p. 150).

Lenin was not alone in regarding the moderate socialists as having sold out to the capitalists and in believing that any agreement was impossible. But pressure for a more left wing coalition continued. It had been brought to a head by Vikzhel, the railway union, which threatened to withhold access to the railways from any political party which tried to rule alone. The Menshevik-controlled post and telegraph union and the printers backed Vikzhel, and Lenin, faced with a concerted opposition from the vital transport and communications unions, began to take more seriously the possibility of persuading the Left SRs to join the government. There is little doubt that both he and Trotsky would have preferred to rule alone. Lenin had said on 1 November that 'our present slogan is no compromises, a homogenous Bolshevik government' (Daniels, 1960, p. 65), and Trotsky had proclaimed with fine rhetoric to the Soviet that the only coalition they needed was with the garrison. Nevertheless alliance with the Left SRs would bring considerable tactical advantages. It would enable the new government to claim to represent the peasantry and thus the overwhelming majority of the population, it would partially satisfy the constant demands for revolutionary unity of the socialist groups, and it might help to solve the looming problem of the Constituent Assembly. It was also, for Lenin, vastly preferable to a coalition with the Mensheviks. The agreement was finally consolidated on 12 December when the Left SRs joined Sovnarkom, taking the portfolios of agriculture and justice but remaining as junior partners. The Congress of Soviets was enlarged by merging it with the separate Congress of Peasant Soviets and including a higher representation from the army and the trade unions. It made the Bolshevik majority on the Central Executive Committee less strong, but it was already apparent that real power was with Sovnarkom.

The agreement was greeted with relief by representatives of grassroots organizations. Resolutions from factory committees, from the army, from Moscow and from provincial towns all made it clear that, although soviet power was popular, what was wanted was for 'revolutionary democracy' to unite, end factional strife, support the Bolsheviks and form a socialist government to solve the problems of the country and avoid civil war. Workers and soldiers might support October and vote for the Bolsheviks in elections, but this did not necessarily imply support for one-party rule, or indeed for Bolshevik policies once these became known. As one resolution from the Moscow metal workers put it, 'we are for Soviet power but against power to one party' (Koenker, 1981, p. 227). Kronstadt again best illustrates the situation. The sailors might provide much of the armed force the Bolsheviks needed, although as individuals those sailors might be anarchist or SR Maximalist, but in Kronstadt itself the Bolsheviks remained in a minority on the town soviet. As late as January 1918 the SR Maximalist chairman of the Kronstadt soviet won a majority for a resolution that party criteria were not applicable in elections. Kronstadt was only Bolshevized, from the outside and by force, in June 1918, but it was none the less hailed as the pride and joy of the Russian revolution. In provincial towns the local soviet assumed power after October, often with a non-Bolshevik majority. The bulk of the population was slow to realize that to the Bolsheviks the revolution meant more than the slogans of 1917.

Many Bolsheviks, including Lenin, believed, however, that party policies and popular aspirations would coexist in practice without much trouble. After all, in Bolshevik theory the party was merely the vanguard of the class, the politically conscious element of the proletariat, and could not act against the interests of that class. Now that capitalism had been overthrown, problems would be solved fairly easily. The idea that basic conflicts could arise between the people and 'their' party was inconceivable to most Bolsheviks, and Lenin in the enthusiasm of 1917 shared this attitude for some months. The question of the relationship between the people and a revolutionary state had been the subject of Lenin's major, if unfinished, work of 1917. Following on from the work of the Bolshevik leader and theorist N. I. Bukharin, whose *Towards a Theory of the Imperialist State* greatly influenced him, Lenin's *State and Revolution*, worked on in Finland before October, boldly considered the necessity of destroying the bourgeois state through a popular uprising. Lenin, however, despite apparent anarchist overtones in the work, was not an anarchist. The bourgeois state, having reached, through an imperialist war, the final stage of monopoly capitalism, would give way not directly to full socialism but to the transitional stage of the dictatorship of the proletariat. This would involve a revolutionary government, to eliminate the bourgeoisie, but there was no clear-cut Marxist blueprint for what that state would be like. Throughout 1917 and the first weeks of 1918 Lenin constantly referred to the Paris Commune as a model, and the term 'the commune state' was used more frequently than the 'dictatorship of the proletariat' in those first few months. Power was to go to the workers through armed militias and through popularly elected soviets and committees at local level. As one commissar told John Reed, the new government would be 'a loose organization sensitive to the popular will as expressed through the Soviets, allowing local forces full play' (Reed, 1960, p. 68).

Lenin observed in *State and Revolution* that the aim was 'an immense expansion of democracy which for the first time becomes democracy for the poor, democracy for the people'. As the party, acting as an educative vanguard, and Sovnarkom established a class dictatorship from above, so the masses would run society from below. Numerous party cadres went to work for the Petrograd Soviet and in local soviets, and initially the party took a low profile giving 'complete freedom to the creative faculties of the masses' (*CW*, 1964, vol. 26, p. 261). Lenin recalled telling a delegation of workers and peasants, 'you are the power, do all you want to do, take all you want. We shall support you' (ibid., p. 468). In *State and Revolution* he had seen the final stages of capitalism as marked by mechanization and simplification of economic and governmental processes to such an extent that ordinary people would be able to run things themselves. Specialists were unnecessary, and it was a common belief that if workers served on committees in large numbers there could be no bureaucratization. Lenin

51

certainly believed at this time that the slide into economic ruin could be halted and socialism built by massive popular involvement at all levels, an attitude which brought him close to the left wing of his party.

It is false to see this libertarian approach as either anarchist utopianism or as quite foreign to the rest of Lenin's thought, but he gave far greater emphasis to it in 1917 than at any other time, and the first decrees of soviet power reflect this as much as they fulfil the promises of 1917. One extreme example was the 'Declaration of the Rights of the People of Russia', which gave complete national determination to the peoples of the empire 'up to the succession and the formation of an independent state' (McCauley, 1975, p. 192). As the Bolsheviks did not control large parts of the country, this may be seen as propaganda, but it reflects the faith that there was community of interest among the vast majority and that the masses would recognize their vanguard party and support it – an attitude that permeates Trotsky's *History* and John Reed's *Ten Days that Shook the World*.

The Decree on Workers' Control on 14 November was fully in line with this spirit. Far from the Bolsheviks restricting workers' control once they came to power, as anarchist historians claim, the decree, drafted by Lenin himself, was a very libertarian document. Indeed, the original draft, drawn up by factory committee leaders, was rejected by Lenin as too concerned to establish a central economic apparatus. (Vesenkha, the Supreme Economic Council, was established on 1 December.) Although stressing the Bolshevik definition of *Kontrol* in the sense of supervision, a matter essentially, as Lenin said, of inspection and accounting, the decree defined it very broadly. The factory committees were given the right to control all aspects of production, including finance, and their decisions were to be binding on managers. It did not give direct management to the committees, although in the post-October chaos some factory committees, especially those outside the capital, took it in this light and the factory committee Central Council encouraged the widest possible interpretation of their powers. The conflicts came less between the new government and the factory committees than between different sections of the party. The left wing stressed full workers' management as the ideal, while the trade unions and the party moderates wished to limit the movement. The demand for nationalization came from below as the revolution and wider workers' powers failed to improve the economy. By the time the factory committees were brought under trade-union control in the spring, many were not opposed to the move. By March Lenin was advocating state capitalism and 'state workers' control', meaning increased centralization and factory management in the hands of one man appointed from the centre, not a factory committee.In the end the factory committees were to get nationalization of industry but not workers' control on the factory floor, which they had seen as its essential accompaniment.

The Decree on Land abolished all private property in land and placed it at the disposal of peasant committees, pending the convocation of the Constituent Assembly. It also laid down that peasant soviets should ensure order and prevent damage. In practice, however, the decree merely sanctioned a movement which was already under way and over which the Bolsheviks had a minimum of control. Lenin, however, believed that the peasants had to be allowed to take the land themselves. He interpreted what was happening in the countryside as a class war between poor peasants and kulaks (rich peasants), in the course of which the poor peasant majority would learn to appreciate their community of interest with the proletariat, supply the towns and support the revolution. Since April 1917 he had been urging the retention of the biggest estates as model collective farms through which the poor peasants could be taught socialist attitudes. This assumption of a natural tie between the proletariat and the mass of the peasantry was one of the gambles involved in the revolution. The plan for model collective farms failed from the beginning; where land was saved from universal distribution, the new farms were looted and their machinery destroyed.

Although by December, after the decrees on land and peace, many peasant soviets in new elections voted Bolshevik, there is no indication that Lenin's analysis had been correct. Towns were not supplied; what conflict there was in the villages was less a class one among the peasantry than a war between town and country, and the preservation of the commune and the levelling effects of an egalitarian redistribution militated against capitalist development. Peasant soviets could not compete with the commune, and the central government found it as difficult to control the village as its predecessors had done. Bolshevik agitators and organizers, who descended on the countryside like a plague of locusts after October, caused much hostility, and by December factories were sending requisition squads into the villages to seize grain hoarded by their peasant brothers. The law on the Socialization of Land in February 1918 set up poor peasant committees (*kombedy*) to work with government agencies, but *kombedy* were often composed of returned workers rather than local peasants, and the commune united against them, as the villages united against the towns. As the proletariat and their ex-masters came from the towns seeking food in exchange for goods the peasants drove a hard bargain. There was little sign either of class conflict in the villages or of the peasant–proletarian solidarity Lenin had taken for granted.

The Decree on Peace was the first decree to be issued by the new regime. Essentially it merely called on all participants to end the war on the basis of no annexations and announced that Russia was withdrawing from the conflict. It opened the way for separate negotiations with Germany, but its first result was to encourage those soldiers still at the front to negotiate cease-fires and then desert. As such it completed the disintegration of the old army. The soldiers' committees, many still loyal to the Petrograd Soviet and in favour of an all-socialist government, were reconstructed by Bolshevik activists and local MRCs, at the front and in local garrison towns. An army, like the police or a bureaucracy, was seen by the Bolsheviks as part of the control mechanism of a capitalist society. Under socialism these organizations would be merged into the armed population. The Red Guards were to be the model of the army of the future, a workers' militia, voluntary, elected and decentralized.

The parts of the army still remaining by the New Year were concentrated in the south and were not under Bolshevik influence; the rest had demobilized themselves. When the next major controversy in the party broke over the peace treaty of Brest-Litovsk, this fact was to be an important part of Lenin's calculations. The only soldiers still available were not necessarily reliable, and it was better to accept the treaty, however harsh its terms, and give the revolution at home time to consolidate itself. Internal considerations, for Lenin, were paramount. To the Left Communists led by Bukharin, however, the international revolution took precedence over all else. One of their number, the Bolshevik feminist Alexandra Kollontai, who was Commissar for Social Welfare, resigned her commissariat over the issue and was even prepared for the Russian revolution to be sacrificed, if necessary, for the higher cause. The left would not accept that the peace propaganda now meant that a revolutionary war was impossible. Lenin himself had said that only a European revolution would enable Russia to move to socialism and had believed that Russia, as the weakest link in the capitalist chain, would start the process. Now to strengthen German imperialism by a shameful peace was unthinkable to the left.

Trotsky, as in October, took a middle position, that of 'neither war, nor peace'. In charge of the negotiations, he played for time, writing the first volume of his *History* at Brest and sending out revolutionary appeals across Europe. However, once the Germans broke off negotiations in February and advanced, the logic of Lenin's position became obvious, although again it needed his threat of resignation to get the Central Committee to agree. The treaty of Brest-Litovsk, signed on 3 March, lost the infant regime large areas of the Ukraine as well as Poland and the Baltic states. These lost western territories included much of Russia's industry and raw materials. It has been calculated that three-quarters of Russia's iron and steel, 26 per cent of her railway network, 26 per cent of her population and much of the most fertile soil of the empire were given over to Germany. The treaty, and the opposition to it inside Russia, made civil war inevitable, but it did have one advantage in Lenin's eyes – it ended the unwanted coalition with the Left SRs, who left Sovnarkom. The Bolsheviks were now on their own.

If the army was to be abolished, so was the police. Police functions also passed to workers' militias, Red Guards and revolutionary tribunals elected by the local soviets. In a situation where almost everyone was armed and guns could be picked up in the markets, criminal elements percolated easily into such organizations. Revolutionary justice was a violent and arbitrary proceeding; an accusation of being a *burzhui* (a bourgeois) was enought to cause arrest or a lynching. Lenin actively encouraged such rudimentary forms of class warfare. The Decree on the Courts abolished the existing legal system, and in December Lenin launched a campaign to incite the population to use terror against the bourgeoisie and anti-Soviet elements. Despite the fact that the Second Congress of Soviets had again abolished the death penalty, Lenin constantly called for speculators and looters to be shot on the spot and hostages to be taken and killed. The use of terror against class enemies, starting with the Kadets, was a constant source of argument in the Soviet's CEC. On 1 December Trotsky justified the use of terror by reference to the Jacobins and the logic of class war. 'There is nothing immoral in the proletariat finishing off a class which is collapsing; that is its right', Trotsky declared (Keep, 1979, p. 177). This was before the Cheka was established later that month as a political police force to combat counter-revolution and sabotage. The existence of such an 'extradordinary commission', initially purely an investigating agency without judicial or punitive powers, was typical of the period. It was at first accountable only to Lenin and was certainly not concerned with law in the 'bourgeois' sense of the term. As its first head, Felix Dzerzhinsky, explained in June 1918, 'The public and the press misunderstand the character and tasks of our commission. They imagine the struggle waged against Counter Revolution to be on the plane of normal state life, and consequently they wail about courts of law, about guarantees, about inquiries, investigators etc. ... We stand for organized terror – this should be frankly stated' (Leggett, 1981, p. 68).

The general lawlessness of the period was heightened by anarchist 'expropriation' squads and hooligan gangs acting to eliminate such bourgeois manifestations as private property. Kronstadt launched itself into an orgy of 'socialization' measures, with its soviet taking possession of shops, banks and even saunas, while private houses were requisitioned and divided among the poor and homeless and placed in the charge of housing committees. Pasternak graphically describes one such incident in *Dr Zhivago*. Another major problem of the first few weeks was alcohol, as the cellars of the Winter Palace and large houses were looted, and drastic measures had to be taken to end what became known as the wine pogroms.

October brought to fruition the class polarization of society which had been developing for many years. For those on the wrong side of the class divide, October changed life drastically as February had not. Not only did the propertied classes reject Bolshevism, but so did the bulk of the Russian intelligentsia. The writer Gorky, whose opposition newspaper was the last to survive the press censorship, attacked the Bolsheviks as destroyers of culture and civilization, and spent much of his time trying to rescue intellectuals from arrest and starvation, and libraries and art treasures from destruction.

There were immediate strikes of civil and municipal servants, teachers and white-collar workers, leaving snow unswept, rubbish uncollected and schools shut. New municipal elections were called, to be boycotted by all parties except the far left. Newly appointed commissars found their offices barred against them, to the distress of those, like Kollontai, who were reluctant to use force. One of the first acts of the regime was to declare the Kadets 'enemies of the people'. Their leaders were arrested and two were killed by Red Guards, and their newspapers were closed. The press ban was soon extended to moderate socialist newspapers but proved easier to announce than to enforce for the first few months. Certainly political opposition was not absent, and all opposition parties except the Mensheviks were prepared to use force or the threat of it, but there was no co-ordination among them, and in any case they all assumed that the regime could not last. It was still believed that it was the Constituent Assembly which was to become the legal, elected authority.

The Bolsheviks had since April been in the forefront of demands that the Assembly should be convened, and both the land decree and that setting up Sovnarkom referred to it as the final arbiter. As the results of the elections came in, however, and it became clear that the Bolsheviks had only a quarter of the votes, the question of what to do about it became pressing. Before April Lenin had scornfully rejected parliamentarianism, but he recognized that the issue had popular support, and moderate Bolsheviks were reluctant to dispense with it. The Left SRs used its convocation as a condition of joining the government, but ironically also made its closure possible by joining the Bolshevik walkout of the Assembly when they realized they could not jointly control it. In his *Theses on the Constituent Assembly* Lenin argued that, if the Left SRs had existed as a separate party at the time of the election arrangements, the peasants would have voted for them and the result would have been more radical. But the real argument was spelt out by the decree dissolving the Assembly after only one day: 'the old bourgeois parliament is effete and incompatible with the aims of realizing socialism. It is not general national institutions but only class institutions which can overcome the resistance of the propertied classes and lay the foundations of a socialistic society' (Bunyan and Fisher, 1934, p. 385). Trotsky announced to the Third All-Russian Congress of Soviets, which met to sanction the closure, 'we have trampled underfoot the principles of democracy for the sake of the loftier principles of a social revolution' (Tyrkova-Williams, 1919, p. 325). Socialism and parliamentary democracy had become opposing concepts. The soviets, it was argued, represented a higher type of revolutionary democracy.

There were attempts to save the Constituent Assembly. The SRs formed a committee for its defence, and a demonstration in the capital at its opening on 5 January was planned to coincide with an attempt to oust the government, but the SRs were reluctant to use force and the affair was badly mishandled. The demonstration, which included many workers, was shot at by the Bolsheviks, and Gorky furiously compared the resulting deaths to Bloody Sunday in 1905. The force behind the dispersion of the Constituent Assembly came, yet again, from Kronstadt. The sailors, including many anarchists, not only guarded the Tauride Palace but thronged the public galleries with, as one eyewitness put it, 'bandoliers of cartridges draped coquettishly across their shoulders and grenades hanging obtrusively from their belts' (Steinberg, 1930, p. 69). The Bolsheviks presented the Assembly with a 'Declaration of the Rights of Toiling and Exploited Peoples', by which it was asked to recognize and approve the new government and to disband itself. When Chernov, as chairman, refused, the government parties withdrew, and shortly afterwards the Assembly was shut, 'as the guards were tired'. By 6 January the leaders of non-Bolshevik Russia were faced with the choice of capitulation or civil war.

Protests at home followed, but it was in Europe that most opposition to the closure was voiced, not all of it from hostile sources. Warnings from socialists like Rosa Luxemburg that press censorship and the end of free elections would lead to bureaucratic despotism discouraged many socialist parties from seeing Bolshevism as a model to follow. They also encouraged a siege mentality in the new regime – a mentality to be strengthened as opposition turned into full-scale civil war by the spring of 1918.

4 The Civil War and War Communism, 1918–1920

By the early spring of 1918 it was clear to Lenin, if not yet to all other Bolshevik leaders, that hopes of a 'commune state' and revolutionary self-government from below were going to have to be postponed. Lenin's speeches began to emphasize party organization and discipline over popular self-government. By 1920 there was a noticeable contrast in tone from 1917 in party proclamations and writings. In 1918 works written about the revolution, like Trotsky's *History of the Russian Revolution to Brest-Litovsk* and John Reed's *Ten Days that Shook the World*, had stressed popular spontaneity. By 1920 Trotsky, in *Terrorism and Communism*, was writing that the dictatorship of the proletariat involved 'the most ruthless form of the state, which embraces the life of the citizens authoritatively in every direction' (1921, p. 157). The other main Bolshevik theorist, Bukharin, came to this view later than Lenin and Trotsky, and in stark contrast to his Left Communism days was to produce, also in 1920, the clearest justification for state control in *The Economics of the Transition Period*. As the civil war developed, Sovnarkom increased its dominance over the CEC of the Soviet, and later the party's Politburo took precedence over Sovnarkom. All over the country, party cells imposed control over local soviets.

The economic crisis of the last period of the Provisional Government had not been alleviated by workers' control and a Soviet government. By the spring of 1918 the rapid deterioration of the economy was causing opposition to the new regime. In the countryside grain requisitioning, Bolshevik agitators and the *kombedy* were all unpopular, and the poor peasant committees were abandoned as a failure in November 1918. More serious for the Bolsheviks were growing signs of disillusionment among the proletariat. Workers' control of industry, where it happened, was less a cause of economic chaos than a response to it, but it did not help the overall situation. The peasantry proved unwilling to supply the towns without getting something in return; the transport system collapsed, and the Bolsheviks did not control the wheat-rich areas of the south and the Ukraine. By the end of February 1918 the bread ration in Petrograd was at an all-time low of 50 grams. The demobilization of the army after December 1917 added to the urban misery. Over 70 per cent of Russia's industry was by then geared to the war effort, and the cease-fire created havoc. Large-scale factory closures and redundancies in the armaments factories led to massive unemployment and, as the Bolsheviks moved the capital to Moscow, Petrograd was again most vulnerable to economic hardship and the fear of enemy attack. Victor Serge describes the town when he arrived in 1919. 'We were entering a world frozen to death. ... It was the metropolis of cold, of hunger, of hatred, of endurance' (Serge, 1963, p. 70). H. G. Wells, visiting the following year, described it as a ghost town.

By the end of 1920 the proletariat, the class the revolution was about, had shrunk to only half its pre-revolutionary size. Petrograd lost 60 per cent of its workforce by April 1918, and one million people had left the city by that June. In Russia as a whole the urban proletariat decreased from 3.6 million in January 1917 to 1.4 million two years later. Starving and unemployed workers left the towns to return to the villages, to join the Red Army, or to enter the ever-growing ranks of the bureaucracy. Hardest hit were the large, state-owned metallurgical factories employing the very section of the working class which had provided the Bolsheviks with the core of their support in 1917. The Vyborg district of Petrograd saw its population fall from 69,000 to 5,000 by the summer of 1918.

The result was that within six months of the revolution significant sections of the proletariat began to oppose Bolshevik power, making coercion inevitable against the workers and peasants as well as the bourgeoisie. Both the closing of the Constituent Assembly and the treaty of Brest-Litovsk aroused protests from factories. An Emergency Representative Assembly of Factory Representatives led a successful, if illegal, existence in Petrograd with Menshevik and SR backing from March to July 1918, with strong support among the skilled workers of large concerns like the Putilov factory. It passed resolutions in favour of a Constituent Assembly, for new soviet elections, for a free press, even for the overthrow of Sovnarkom, and called a general strike, but with little success. Mensheviks and SRs enjoyed a resurgence of support in local soviets throughout the country. However, when new soviet elections were held in June, the Bolsheviks, now renamed the Communist Party, again emerged triumphant. They were still associated with soviet power, and the soviets were still seen as the workers' institutions. That fact, as well as the willingness to use coercion, kept Lenin in power. By January 1918 he was referring to strikers as hooligans, and by May groups of protesting workers calling for food and work were shot by Red Guards outside Petrograd.

Political opposition also resurfaced, this time from the extreme left. The anarchist headquarters in Moscow was disarmed in April after a series of anarchist attacks on government institutions. The Left SRs, who left Sovnarkom as a result of the treaty of Brest-Litovsk, turned to open opposition and terrorism. Their first victim was Count Mirbach, the German ambassador, on 6 July; the head of the Cheka, Dzerzhinsky, who had gone to investigate, was seized, and Left SRs, still operating inside the Cheka, staged an abortive attempt to seize Moscow. At the same time an SR uprising led by Savinkov, who had been General Kornilov's commissar in the summer of 1917, seized Yaroslavl but failed to hold it after ferocious fighting. But, if SR uprisings failed, their terrorist attempts were more successful. On 30 August an unsuccessful assassination attempt left Lenin badly wounded. Over the period of two months that summer two Bolshevik party leaders were killed and plots were uncovered against two others. By now such activities were part of the civil war in which the SRs threw in their lot energetically with the anti-Bolshevik or White cause. In some senses the civil war dated from October with the military resistance of General Krasnov. Lenin certainly saw civil war, in the sense of a class war against the bourgeoisie, as part of a revolution. Nevertheless, according to Bolshevik theory, the bourgeoisie was too weak in Russia to offer great resistance, and the inevitable European revolution would make any threat of foreign intervention impossible. However, Bolshevik policies themselves heightened the possibility of civil war. The refusal of coalition, the closing of the Constituent Assembly and the treaty of Brest-Litovsk all led to political opponents taking up arms with greater or lesser enthusiasm.

Most historians date the outbreak of full-scale hostilities from May 1918 with the revolt of the Czech legion and the British occupation of Murmansk and Archangel. The Czechs had been captured on the Austrian front and were in prisoner-of-war camps in the Urals when an independent Czech state was established which declared its support for the Allies. Negotiations took place to remove the legion from Russia via Vladivostok so that it could fight on the western front. A fracas with Hungarian prisoners and a Bolshevik attempt to disarm the legion led to a mutiny, and the Czechs took over control of the all-important Trans-Siberian railway. While they remained a fighting force, they dominated the railway and large stretches of the Urals and the Volga. With prisoner-of-war mercenary units trying to fight their way out of Russia, foreign intervention, partisan guerrilla movements and local separatists, the civil war was far more than a straight Red-versus-White struggle for power in Moscow. Nor was it in any real sense a class struggle. It was a war of fluctuating alliances and individual loyalties, and it divided families as easily as classes. It also devastated what was left of the Russian economy, and its chaos and savagery can best be understood from literature and memoirs.

The White cause was a precarious alliance of defeated politicians and discredited generals. After October Kornilov was freed by his guards and fled south to join General Alekseev's Volunteer Army on the Don. Kornilov himself was killed in a minor campaign almost immediately, Alekseev died, and so command passed to General A. I. Denikin, who, throughout the war, declared his support for an eventual re-election of a Constituent Assembly: 'The army will stand guard over civil liberties until the day when the master of the Russian land, the Russian people, can express its will through the elections of a Constituent Assembly' (Denikin, 1921, vol. 2, pp. 198–9). It should be pointed out, perhaps, that few Whites wanted a return of the monarchy, even before the execution of the royal family in July, although, if the Constituent Assembly remained the official goal, many certainly felt the need for an indefinite period of military dictatorship first. As the empire fell apart, many national minority areas declared their independence, rejected Bolshevism and set up their own locally elected assemblies. The Kadets and moderate socialists, as they joined the soldiers after the closure of the Constituent Assembly, had two problems. The first was how to utilize this local anti-Bolshevism and preserve the idea of democracy despite the military imperatives of war, and the second was how to keep Russia united against the separatist tendencies of the provinces.

The Kadet leadership was prepared to abandon the Constituent Assembly, at least for the foreseeable future, and to rely on military dictatorship to defeat Lenin, and they gave political respectability to the Volunteer Army. However, they repeated on the Don the mistakes of the Provisional Government: basic social change and democratic rights were again to be delayed until the war was over and the Constituent Assembly re-elected. General Denikin's conservative land policies lost him peasant support; land reform was not implemented, and landlords were promised the return of land seized by the peasantry. Moreover, Denikin's insistence on 'Russia one and indivisible' alienated the nationalists. The Volunteer Army operated across Cossack country and although the Don Cossacks at first co-operated they did so reluctantly. As any reader of M. Sholokhov's *And Quiet Flows the Don* will know, the Cossacks' aim was local autonomy, not a united Russia. The Whites would be welcomed against the threat of Bolshevism but would not be helped to re-establish central control, and the Cossacks were quite prepared to seek German protection to ensure their local self-government.

The Volunteer Army was only one bastion of what one might call right-wing opposition to Moscow. A more successful Kadet venture was a much publicized and well-supported, but short-lived, 'model' constitutional government in the Crimea, one of the very rare examples of Kadet-SR collaboration. Siberia had claimed autonomy before October, and Omsk at first had a democratic government controlled by locally elected members of the Constituent Assembly, mostly SRs. However the town soon became the centre for Admiral Kolchak, probably the most serious threat the Bolsheviks faced. Kolchak was to declare himself Supreme Ruler in November 1918. In the north-west, the Bolsheviks faced a motley and squabbling collection of Balts, Finns and White partisans as well as the continuing German threat from the independent, right-wing German leader, von der Goltz, who dominated the Baltic. In the Far East, White generals acting like Chinese warlords controlled the Chinese Eastern railway and the borders of Manchuria and Mongolia.

Moderate socialist opposition to Bolshevism also operated on the fringes of the empire but usually independently from Kadets and right-wing forces. Whereas the Kadets had gone to the Don after Jaunary 1918, the SRs re-established the Constituent Assembly at Samara (the Komuch) and claimed to be the legal government of Russia. By putting into practice locally their promises of land reform and local autonomy, they gained peasant support and received military backing from the Czechs. But they wished to be the central government, not a local one. In September 1918 at a state conference at Ufa they merged with the Siberian government of Omsk and local Muslim assemblies to form a Directory, which, like Siberian democracy, was to fall victim to Kolchak. Separate SR elected governments operated briefly, and with some popular backing, in north Russia and in the Ukraine, where the elected assembly, or Rada, was dominated by local SRs. The Rada appealed for German aid against the invading Bolsheviks in the early spring of 1918, only to be abandoned by them when Germany occupied the Ukraine after Brest-Litovsk. The Germans established a Russian general, Skoropadsky, as supreme ruler or Hetman, to be puppet dictator. In his brief rule he fought not only the Bolsheviks but also the Ukrainian nationalists under Simon Petlyura who were attempting to restore the moderate socialist Rada, and Nestor Makhno's peasant guerrillas. Kiev changed hands so often that its bewildered occupants were not always aware which army was threatening the city at any given time. Meanwhile the Mensheviks had retreated to their stronghold of Georgia, where, despite their socialist and internationalist aspirations, they ran a democratic national government with considerable success. A parliament was established consisting initially of elected delegates to the Constituent Assembly, but new elections were held in 1919 giving the Mensheviks an overwhelming majority.

The civil war was never a purely Russian affair, and in all almost a dozen nationalities were involved. The Germans occupied the Ukraine until November 1918 and supplied separatist movements of various political shades from the Baltic to the Caucasus. The British and French first discussed intervention in December 1917, when rough spheres of interest were mapped out. Soviet historiography has portrayed the intervention as an imperialist plot without which White resistance would have been short-lived. In fact, the initial Allied concern was with the war and the preservation of the eastern front, and they would have been prepared to consider recognizing the Bolsheviks if they had remained in the war. Several attempts were made to negotiate with Lenin, the Bruce-Lockhart mission and that by William Bullitt being the best known. There were vast quantities of war supplies stored at the northern ports, and the French in particular were concerned to retrieve some of the huge sums invested in Russian industry. Both powers had large numbers of personnel in Russia. Intervention initially meant channelling supplies to the Volunteer Army and anyone thought likely to fight the Germans. Military involvement began in May 1918, but by the end of the year it was clear that full-scale fighting would not be tolerated by the war-weary western soldiers or by public opinion at home. The French in particular saw mutinies among their troops. After the armistice in the west the motive for intervention changed to a more anti-Bolshevik stance, especially on the part of Churchill, but little serious planning seems to have gone into the venture. Indeed, the scheme to link troops from Archangel with the Czech legion on the Volga suggests that no one had looked at a map. This is not to deny that foreign intervention was a threat to the new regime. The British occupied not just the northern ports but parts of Transcaucasia and briefly Baku, the French invaded from Odessa, the Japanese launched a straightforward attempt at annexation of the Far-Eastern territories, and Vladivostok was overrun by international missions, including the Americans. White armies relied heavily on foreign supplies, but nevertheless it is not easy to argue that foreign intervention was fundamental to the White cause, although it probably prolonged the war. In some ways it was a disadvantage, since reliance on foreign support kept White armies tied to the edges of the empire in easy reach of a port.

The crucial year was 1919. On the defence everywhere at the beginning of the year, by the end the Reds had control of all fronts. Generals Denikin and Yudenich were turned back in October, Denikin only 250 miles from Moscow and Yudenich on the outskirts of Petrograd. Omsk was evacuated by Kolchak the following month, and he was executed by the Bolsheviks after they occupied Irkutsk in January 1920. By then it looked as if the war was over, but 1920 brought two new crises. The Russo-Polish war was a separate affair. Lenin's reaction to foreign intervention had been the foundation of the Third International (Comintern), and hopes rose in 1919 for a European revolution. However, the Polish leader Marshal Pilsudski saw the civil war as an excuse for a newly independent Poland to revive national glories by extending her territories in the east, and he invaded Russia. This time, by contrast with 1918, it was Lenin who overruled Trotsky's hesitations and insisted on launching a revolutionary war into Poland. Instead of unleashing a proletarian uprising, however, the Red Army succeeded only in arousing Polish nationalism, and the advance was halted before Warsaw. The resulting armistice was signed just in time for the Red Army to turn south and to defeat General Wrangel's last-ditch uprising in the Crimea. Wrangel had succeeded Denikin as commander in south Russia and was the last of the White generals. His defeat ended the attempts by the anti-Bolshevik forces to regain power.

The White movement was deeply split – between socialists and liberals, politicians and soldiers, centralists and local separatists. Some groups looked to Germany, others remained loyal to the Allies. Not infrequently conflicts were as fierce between different White armies as between them and the Reds. The Bolsheviks, by moving the capital to Moscow, controlled the all-important railway network, and communication between, say, Kolchak and Denikin often relied on a man on horseback or the telegraph line via Paris or London. Military advances were not co-ordinated, and the Bolsheviks were able to defeat their enemies one by one. Support for the Whites was initially far from negligible. Outside the Bolshevik strongholds of the capital and a few industrial centres, support for the Constituent Assembly remained strong – and the church was overwhelmingly anti-Bolshevik. However, with the exception of the SRs at Samara, the Whites lost peasant support by refusing to implement land reform and making it clear that the landlords would return. The Volunteer Army, at first composed predominantly of officers, quickly ceased to be voluntary; and conscription and the White terror caused widespread hostility. The brutality of the White armies, their wholesale shooting of prisoners and their encouragement of anti-Jewish pogroms were well documented and widely publicized by the Bolsheviks.

But the peasants' attitude to all armies was largely hostile, and White terror was not necessarily worse than proletarian requisitioning of grain and Red terror. Having obtained peace and land, peasants merely wanted to be left alone. On conscription into any army they deserted as soon as possible, only to find themselves forced into service by the next army to occupy their neighbourhood. Armies which did get peasant support, although not necessarily without coercion, were the so-called greens: peasant guerrillas and partisans, of whom the most famous group was Makhno's anarchist army in the Ukraine. Makhno was distinctive because of his anarchist beliefs and his success. Militarily he was a guerrilla fighter of genius, and the Bolsheviks were prepared in the short term to co-operate with him against the Whites. Trotsky described him as a greater threat than Denikin because 'the Makhno movement developed in the depths of the masses and aroused the masses themselves against us' (Voline, 1974, p. 124). Makhno's undeniable support, however, does not prove that the Ukrainian peasants were natural followers of an anarchist ideology, but rather that they wanted control of their own land against all outside interference, Red or White. This appeal was valid for all partisan groups.

The Bolsheviks could not rely on automatic popular support. Their victory in the civil war must be explained by other factors. Although the most productive grain-growing areas were in White hands, the new government controlled not only the railway network but also the main industrial centres. The party had a unity of purpose denied to its enemies and a potential for ruthlessness and organization which it now proved fully determined to use. Above all the new Bolshevik army was fashioned into a fighting force far more effective than that of its opponents. It was created at the very end of 1917 to defend Petrograd against the Germans. Its original core consisted of Red Guards and Kronstadt sailors, supplemented by proletarian volunteers. From the beginning the army was a source of constant friction within the party. As Lenin's writings of 1917 testify, Bolshevik theorists regarded armies as instruments of capitalist oppression. The left wing of the party was deeply suspicious of a standing army of any type. During the Brest-Litovsk crisis Bukharin had argued that a traditional army was not necessary for revolutionary warfare, and that guerrilla partisan warfare by the armed people themselves could replace it.

Trotsky's assumption of command of the new Red Army in March 1918 intensified the conflict. Trotsky was convinced that to win the civil war what was needed was an army of the old kind – regular, organized, highly disciplined and professionally run. He was to create exactly that. In stark contrast to the post-February revolution experience, all elected soldiers' committees were abolished, as were elected party cells in the army. The new Red Army conscripted peasants and took hostages and shot them. The death penalty was reintroduced and used, even for party members, for cowardice and desertion. Officers were appointed, not elected, and four-fifths of them were ex-tsarist officers. To ensure that the army could safely use the professional expertise of these officers, a system of political commissars was established to share command. The commissar was to keep the officer under surveillance and educate him in communist principles. A good literary portrayal of the workings of the system, and its problems, can be found in D. Furmanov's *Chapayev*, an account of a civil war hero by his political commissar which became one of the most popular of all Soviet films in the 1930s. The lack of suitable personnel was, however, a chronic problem, and this often meant that the political commissars were ineffectual intellectuals and not always even party members. The civil war produced some odd assignments. The sending of Isaac Babel, a bespectacled Jewish writer with a horror of shedding blood, to the Polish front as a supply officer with the Red Cossacks was not the best way of educating them in communist ideas.

The party's hostility to the use of professional officers, its commitment to the idea of a militia and its distaste for the ruthless way in which Trotsky managed the army surfaced in March 1919 and again a year later. Lenin, however, supported Trotsky throughout. Although Lenin was never a military leader in the sense that Mao or Castro were to be, he was nevertheless in command of detailed planning and took most of the strategic decisions as chairman of the Supreme Council of Defence. As commander-in-chief Trotsky was given a free hand to speed round the country in his armoured train and, in the process, to make enemies. The Red Army, like the White ones, had its share of personal feuds. The antagonism between Trotsky and Stalin started over the handling of the southern front in 1919. Stalin became a member of the Military Opposition, which called for a greater emphasis on partisan warfare. Zinoviev and Trotsky were also in dispute for much of the civil war.

Trotsky's influence was not confined to the army. Indeed, he came to see the army as a model for all Soviet life to follow during the dictatorship of the proletariat. Good military discipline and administration should also be applied to the economy and could lead the way to a socialist system through a centralist, state-planned economy. The concept of militarization of labour, the transferring of army practices on to the civilian economy, was formally proposed by Trotsky to the party Central Committee in December 1919. The idea was that all adults not already in the ranks of the army should be conscripted under military discipline for labour armies. The following month he also suggested that at the end of the war the standing army should be converted into a militia with its members combining normal work in field or factory and regular military training. Lenin supported the idea of the militarization of labour, and it was accepted at the Ninth Party Congress in March 1920, despite bitter hostility from many sections of the party and from the trade-union movement, whose remaining powers it would have abolished. As a trial run the third army was transformed into the first labour army at the end of the war, and the transport system was also brought under strict military discipline by Trotsky through the Transport Commission (Tsektran). Martial law had been applied to the railways after the Bolsheviks had gained control of the railway union Vikzhel in 1918, and by the following year, with 60 per cent of the locomotive stock out of action and fears that the whole network would collapse, the crisis was such that drastic measures were regarded as necessary. Trotsky, however, certainly saw Tsektran as an example of military organization that other industries could follow.

Although the militarization of labour was never fully implemented, the system of War Communism from the beginning entailed a large degree of centralization, compulsion and discipline. War Communism should not be seen merely as an *ad hoc* reaction to civil war and crisis. Although there was no plan for the creation of a socialist economy, most Bolsheviks, including Lenin, now regarded centralized state control as socialist. War Communism was introduced as a specific policy in the spring of 1918, and once it was established Lenin was reluctant, even at the end of 1920, to abandon it. In *The Immediate Tasks of the Soviet Government*, published in April 1918, Lenin wrote that only by 'the strictest and universal accounting and control of the production and distribution of goods' (*CW*, 1965, vol. 27, p. 241) could the power of the working people maintain itself. The more enthusiastic adherents could even believe that rampant inflation and the collapse of a money economy into a barter system was a symbol of advanced socialist development. War Communism was the heroic age of the revolution. On the economic front everything was subordinated to the war effort. Although it was not immediate party policy in October 1917 to nationalize industry, by 1920 all enterprises, including windmills, were nationalized. All private trade and manufacture were banned, leading to an enormous and indispensable black market. In the countryside War Communism amounted to little more than the forceful requisitioning of grain. Labour discipline was draconian and must have been a considerable shock to a workforce accustomed to the anarchy and freedom of 1917. Workers' control was replaced by appointed managers, and Lenin exhorted everyone that they should 'unquestioningly obey the single will of the leaders of labour' (ibid., p. 269). The bewildered bourgeois could find himself either in charge of his own factory as a specialist or in prison as a class enemy.

A siege economy led to a fortress mentality. Workers were punished for lateness or absenteeism, and the working day was ten or eleven hours. None of this, however, was sufficient to stop the decline of the economy. Industrial output was less than one-seventh of 1913 levels by the end of the war. Novels tell of devastated factories and a demoralized labour force. In F. Gladkov's *Cement* the workers make cigarette lighters to swap for food. Labour discipline was enforced, like much else, by the Cheka. Chekists soon acquired responsibilities far beyond their original brief of opposing sabotage and counter-revolution. The death penalty was reintroduced in July 1918 after the Left SRs, who claimed to have mitigated the Cheka's excesses, withdrew from the institution. As Lenin said, 'a revolutionary who does not want to play the hypocrite cannot dispense with the death penalty' (Leggett, 1981, p.

63). After the attempt on his life the Cheka launched a Red terror. Its victims were not just speculators or saboteurs from the bourgeoisie but included large numbers of workers and peasants. Peasant uprisings were crushed with great ferocity. Concentration camps and forced-labour camps were established to house prisoners, the forerunners of Stalin's Gulag. Hostages were taken and random shootings were common as reprisals. According to the latest western authority on the Cheka, Leggett, deaths directly attributable to the institution amounted to over a quarter of a million by 1924. Thus the state of war was extended to the civilian sphere; Lenin explained that 'what dictatorship means is a state of simmering war, a state of military means of struggle against the enemies of proletarian power' (*CW*, 1964, vol. 26, p. 401). Enemies were defined simply in the terms that 'those not being with us are against us'. Although members of other socialist parties maintained a shadowy existence in the soviets and trade unions, they could be arrested if the Bolsheviks decided that they were acting in a way prejudicial to the revolution.

Not surprisingly the civil war years had far-reaching effects on both society and the party. Peasant revolts erupted throughout the country as the civil war ended and the Whites and the threat of returning landlords retreated. One of the biggest was in the Tambov area between the rivers Don and Volga, where Bolshevik administrative centres and the documents they held were burnt and railway and grain-collecting centres attacked. Stiffened by the presence of army deserters and bandits, the movement involved up to 20,000 people. For the SRs it was a tragic example of popular anti-Bolshevism which came too late for the shattered SR party to take advantage of it. It was, however, probably the Tambov revolt which helped to convince Lenin that concessions would have to be made to the peasantry and that War Communism would have to be ended. Famine was widespread across southern Russia by 1921 after a grain harvest which reached only a little over half of the 1913 levels, and typhoid and cholera reached epidemic proportions.

By 1920 it is probable that what remained of the proletariat was deeply disillusioned with Bolshevik rule. One indication is the sharp fall in proletarian membership of the party. The industrial proletariat by 1920 was predominantly female, unskilled and not able to organize itself. Strikes broke out in several industrial towns, including Petrograd, as the civil war came to an end. Trade unions opposed War Communism and were attacked as syndicalist by Lenin, but the party was aware of its unpopularity with the workers.

Perhaps the biggest impact of these years was on the Communist Party itself. The experiences of civil war and the responsibilities of government had radically altered it. Party members now typically worked in offices rather than in large industrial factories, and in Petrograd by 1920 38 per cent of members were in the army in one capacity or another. The decline in support from the soviets and from the factories was to have profound implications for the nature of the party and the revolution. These years saw several purges of undesirables from the party, and by 1919 the numbers were down to 150,000. After a recruitment drive the party claimed its membership in 1920 to be 600,000, but of these the overwhelming majority had, like N. S. Khrushchev, joined since 1918 and were of peasant background. Not only did they have no knowledge of the hopes and dreams of 1917, but they also knew little if anything of Marx. The relatively democratic atmosphere of the party in the revolutionary year was one of the first casualties of the civil war. After the spring of 1918 the party became increasingly centralized and hierarchical. The central organs, like the newly created Politburo and Orgburo as well as the secretariat, increased their powers. Although local party committees were not abolished, they complained that they were denied the opportunity to debate issues. Until his death in March 1919 Y. M. Sverdlov as party secretary was, apart from Lenin, the linchpin of the whole apparatus. Although there was much consultation in an informal way among the top party leadership, day-to-day decisions were concentrated in the hands of Lenin, Sverdlov and, increasingly, Stalin. The Central Committee met infrequently.

Nevertheless there is little doubt that this increased centralization and discipline was accepted by the vast majority of the party rank and file. The crisis of both the civil war and the economy was accepted as a justification for almost anything, and orders were obeyed. The attitudes of military discipline and obedience percolated into the party's life at all levels. 60,000 Bolsheviks served in the army, and the experience was to leave a lasting mark on them. Indeed, some groups argued for more centralization. Opposition did not come from the rank and file but resulted from divisions in the leadership which surfaced again by 1919. As it became obvious that the civil war would be won, many looked back with longing to the ideals of 1917 and hoped to be able to return to them. Apart from the Military Opposition, the two most important groups were the Democratic Centralists and the Workers' Opposition.

The Democratic Centralists wanted a better balance between democracy and centralism in the workings of the party. They wished to combine greater control from the centre with a return to elected offices and collective decision-making at local levels. They proposed to enable local party organizations to have some check on the Central Committee by regular conferences. At the Eighth Party Congress in March 1919 they were criticized by the leadership for disloyalty, and, although they put forward their ideas again the following year, they also demonstrated their essential loyalty by joining in the attack on the Workers' Opposition as an 'anarcho-syndicalist deviation'.

The Workers' Opposition was more radical and threatening, partly because its leadership had greater standing in the party. It was led by Shlyapnikov, and Alexandra Kollontai wrote its programme. It also had the support of the trade unions and was part of a wider debate on trade-union powers. At a time when Zinoviev calculated that 90 per cent of the trade-union rank and file had Menshevik sympathies, this was serious. The Workers' Opposition showed that for Kollontai and those on the left of the party their faith in the proletariat was undiminished. Kollontai wrote that 'the healthy class instinct of the working masses' should be trusted to 'develop the creative powers in the sphere of economic reconstruction' (Holt, 1977, p. 162). Trade unions, factory committees and other elected workers' bodies should be trusted to run industry themselves and to create socialism. She wanted an All-Russian Congress of Producers and even proposed that every party member should spend three months of every year working in factories and villages – an idea to be revived by the Chinese in the 1960s. It was widely acknowledged by 1920 that some commissars were but old tsarist officials writ large, and the bureaucracy had become a cause of real concern. The solution of the Workers' Opposition was 'wide publicity, freedom of opinion and discussion, the right to criticise within the party and among members of the trade unions' (ibid., p. 196).

By 1921 the Bolshevik leadership was still as deeply divided as ever. At the Tenth Party Congress in March all the old arguments about the nature of the revolution and the relationship of the party to the masses were again to be fought out.

5 The Battle on the Cultural Front, 1917–1921

The debate on the nature of the revolution and on what the 'transitional period' to full communism was to involve was not confined to the political sphere. The Left Communists opposed Lenin on internationalist grounds over the peace of Brest-Litovsk and over the vexed issue of the relationship of the party to the masses in the Workers' Opposition. But one of the most hotly contested areas of debate within the party was on the nature and importance of a 'cultural revolution', and the formation of a new socialist lifestyle.

Moreover, the October revolution occurred in the midst of a period of intense artistic experimentation which pre-dated the First World War and was to continue until the end of the 1920s. The artistic and educational establish-ment had welcomed the February revolution but were hostile to Bolshevism and initially refused to collaborate with the new regime. This left the field open to the avant-garde – young, left-wing artists who, although they were as deeply divided among themselves as were the politicians, quickly saw in the October revolution an unparalleled opportunity to take their radical ideas of art to the people. As the Bolshevik artist and poet V. Mayakovsky wrote in his first *Order to the Army of Art*, 'The streets are our brushes, the squares our palettes.' The battle for the new society had to be fought on the cultural front as well as on the military and economic, and all branches of art and literature were to be pressed into service, from the rewriting of history textbooks now seen as bourgeois, to the use of mass street theatre. The combination of artistic experimentation and intense intellectual debate over cultural matters was to give rise to a period of artistic vigour and utopian dreams in the period of the revolution and the civil war.

Many on the left of the party and in the artistic world plunged with millenarian fervour into the creation of a new society, a new Soviet man, and woman, through a cultural revolution, both in Russia and, as they hoped and expected, across Europe. The utopian undercurrents present in Russian, as in European, nineteenth-century radical thought came to the forefront as the revolution actually occurred. With greater or lesser degrees of commitment, nearly all the major political figures were carried along by it at one time or another. Lenin's writings throughout 1917 and the early part of 1918 concerning the withering away of the state, particularly, but not uniquely, in *State and Revolution*, show that he was not unaffected by the general euphoria, although he strongly rejected suggestions of utopianism. Certainly at that stage he was envisaging, as not too far distant, the final stage of communism when no governmental powers would be necessary in society and the state would cease to exist. Lenin, however, was in this respect by far the most pragmatic of the Bolshevik leaders. Others, including Lunacharsky, Gorky, Bukharin and above all Trotsky, talked frequently in utopian language. Trotsky described the task of the revolution as being to create 'a higher biological type ... a race of supermen'. The average man would 'rise to the level of Aristotle or Goethe or Marx and beyond this ridge new peaks will rise' (Trotsky, 1960, p. 256). In an address to the working class in April 1918 he spoke of creating a 'real paradise on earth for the human race ... for our children and grandchildren and for all eternity'. The revolution was heralded as a fundamental break with the past leading to a new 'bright future', a perfect, good society for the proletariat and ultimately for all mankind. The visual image of the sunrise was a common one in Bolshevik posters. There were no precedents, all was new, and everything was possible. Bukharin's *ABC of Communism*, written for a mass readership in early 1919 as a commentary on the new party programme, is a good example of utopian thinking, and in this it is also stated that 'human culture will climb to new heights never before attained' (Bukharin and Preobrazhensky 1969, p. 121).

But what was this new socialist culture to be like? How was it to be achieved and how urgent was the task? Would it arise of its own accord following the political and economic changes that the revolution was introducing, or was it dependent on education and intellectual endeavour? Above all, could a new proletarian culture itself help to create socialism? These issues were to be the subject of bitter conflicts centred round the newly created Commissariat of the Enlightenment (Narkompros) and its first commissar, Lunacharsky. All Bolshevik leaders recognized the necessity, given the precarious and ill-educated nature of much of their support, to embark on a vast programme of education and propaganda. All members of the party and their supporters (a small minority) in the literary and artistic worlds could agree on the need to utilize literature and art in the creation of socialism and oppose those artists who advocated art for art's sake and the preservation of nineteenth-century 'high' culture as an end in itself. But there the agreements ended. Cultural themes became as much a battleground among the rival factions as politics.

It is important to realize that deep divisions of opinion existed within the party and had done for many years. The left wing of the party had opposed Lenin in cultural matters from at least 1909, when the 'Forward' group around A. A. Bogdanov had established a party school for workers on Capri. Bodganov was Lenin's main rival within the Bolshevik party in the years between 1905 and the First World War, and their views on the nature of revolution and their interpretation of Marxism were very different.

After 1905 the Bogdanovite brand of Bolshevism had been very influential in party circles, and it was to attempt to counter this influence that Lenin had undertaken his only real venture into philosophy with *Materialism and Empiriocriticism*. Bogdanov's ideas stemmed from his willingness to criticize Marx and to blend Marxism with the newer, neo-positivist philosophy of Mach and Avenarius. This led him to emphasize the primacy of the cultural over the political or economic factors in revolution. For Bogdanov, immediate and drastic changes in the social and cultural structure of society could bring about socialism before a suitable economic substructure, in Marx's terms, existed. Art and lifestyle were not merely the reflection of the economic base and thus of the ruling group in society. They were in themselves causative elements in creating a new society. Proletarian culture could fully prevail only in a socialist society, but it could begin under capitalism and be part of the class struggle. As he put it, 'art ... is a most powerful weapon for the organization of collective forces, and in a class society of class forces' (Scheibert, 1971, p. 49).

Collectivity was central to Bogdanov's view of proletarian culture. Indeed, all agreed that socialist society would be collectively organized. The individual, so important to bourgeois culture, would merge into the collective. 'I' would be replaced by 'we' – significantly to become the title of an anti-utopian novel in 1920 by Y. Zamyatin, a rare dissenting voice. Bogdanov had himself given a picture of a future collectivist communist utopia in his pre-revolutionary science-fiction novel *Red Star*. Lunacharsky talked of the individual's becoming immortalized through the collective. Alexandra Kollontai based much of her theory of women's liberation on the development under socialism of co-operative lifestyles, communes, crêches and collective cooking and eating facilities which would enable the break-up of the nuclear family. Like Bogdanov, she believed that the new collective life must be achieved from below by the workers themselves, simultaneously with or even before political power was fully consolidated. She preached a gospel of all forms of individual love, erotic and maternal, being blended into the higher love for the group. Bukharin's *ABC of Communism*, like early Soviet law codes, makes it clear that the individual, as opposed to the group or the class, has no rights. The assumption is obvious: there will be complete unity between the individual will and that of the collective. Only the harmoniously organized collective experience, said Bodganov, would give the new Soviet man 'that grandiose fullness of life of which we, the people of the epoch of contradictions, cannot even form a conception' (ibid., p. 46). This glorification of the collective was to lead to conductorless orchestras, collective poetry and, more seriously, a spate of attempts at communal living and new designs for town planning.

Lenin attacked Bogdanov's whole approach as anti-Marxist idealism. Marxism, he argued, was the only ideology necessary for the new working class. Bogdanov, however, persisted in his attempt to fuse idealist and materialist philosophies into one 'monist' ideology which would abolish the distinctions between matter and spirit, superstructure and substructure. He was also prepared to blend religion and science and to utilize myths to inspire the proletariat, and this line of argument had a strong influence on his brother-in-law, Lunacharsky. Bogdanov's emphasis was increasingly put on science; Lunacharsky, who had worked on millenarianism as a research student, put his emphasis on religion. He was sympathetic to Gorky's anthropocentric, religious definition of Marxism as a god-building philosophy, and like Trotsky envisaged the new society as a world in which men would become gods. Lunacharsky's own plays, *The Magi* and *Ivan Goes to Heaven*, used mystical and religious images. There was no question that the proletariat would become the new elite, but Lunacharsky and Gorky, while believing in the primacy of the cultural revolution, were also anxious to educate the illiterate and the peasantry and were prepared to use folk legends and traditions to forge new legends, myths and heroes. This was not merely a way of appealing to a peasant audience which could be expected to identify with such familiar themes, although this was partly true. As one Proletkult theatre director said, 'dressing the logical and inevitable course of history in the clothes of the fantastic, the mythic and the legendary can achieve great results' (Mgebrov, 1928, pp. 483–4).

The proletarian culture movement (Proletkult) was the channel through which many of Bogdanov's ideas were disseminated during this period. They took from Bodganov, who had criticized Lenin's *What is to be Done?* and since 1904 had advocated that the proletariat should run its own affairs, a belief that the new culture must come from the working class itself. Conceived in the July Days as a cultural offshoot of the factory committees, and holding its first conference only days before the October revolution, Proletkult held itself aloof both from party control and from the influence of bourgeois intellectuals. Like the factory committees themselves, many of Proletkult's activities were spontaneous and had considerable support from the proletariat, and it took time for Lenin to bring it under party control. Moreover, not all party leaders regarded its independent activities as a threat. It was encouraged by Lunacharsky and given the facilities of Narkompros, but he refused to allow it status as the official representative of party attitudes. Indeed, many of his own ideas, including his god-building philosophy and his concern to retain the best of bourgeois art, were anathema to Proletkult. Lunacharsky, who threatened to resign after false reports that the Kremlin had been damaged in the fighting for Moscow during the revolution, agreed with Lenin that any new culture must be built on the best of the old. Even Bogdanov argued for this, saying that hidden collectivist ideas existed in the best of the old art, and some Proletkult studios used the classics, but many members of the organization were anxious that all bourgeois, and indeed peasant, art should be destroyed to make way for the new urban, industrial proletarian culture. Lunacharsky, however, was willing to accede to Proletkult's demands for autonomy from the party and protected it from Lenin's hostility until 1920. Proletkult's leaders argued strongly that, since the new government and its people's commissariats, such as Narkompros, were of mixed class composition, relied on bourgeois experts, and had to consider the interests of the non-proletarian members of society, only Proletkult could concentrate on the proletariat and thus be regarded as the guardian of proletarian culture. This battle was finally lost in 1920 when Lenin subordinated the institution to Narkompros and to party control. Lenin, who attacked what he called Proletkult's 'absurd ideas' at the extramural conference in May 1919, increasingly associated them not just with his old enemy Bogdanov but with opposition groups in the party, like the Workers' Opposition, and indeed outside the party. Bogdanov himself was no longer a party member by 1917, and the institution was to some extent a haven for ex-Mensheviks and Left SRs and what Lenin was to call in a wider context the 'infantile disorder' of the left.

Lenin had some cause for concern. Proletkult had 400,000 people attending its studios and workshops by 1920, ran sixteen journals, and its educational and extramural activities rivalled those of Narkompros (for example, whereas Narkompros organized *rabfaks* to bring workers up to university level, Proletkult ran a proletarian university), and it was through these institutions that its ideas on the nature of proletarian art emerged. Industry was an obvious starting point for a proletarian culture. Machines were to be a bridge between art and industry; the artist was to become an engineer. The subject matter of the new art was to be the interests and aspirations of the international working class. Metals became muses, standardization and synchronization were heralded as the new lifestyle. One poet wrote a song of iron. Another, Gastev, who later gave up poetry to run an 'institute of work', wrote poems to factory hooters in a collection called *Shock Work Poetry*: 'We all begin together at the identical minute.

A whole million of us take our hammers at the identical second. Our first hammer blows resound in unison. What do the hooters sing of? It is our morning hymn to unity' (Thomson, 1972, p. 83). It is perhaps significant that not even Proletkult, with its desire to destroy the past, could escape from a terminology which still used images such as 'a temple of labour' or 'a hymn to unity'.

Heroes of novels were workers rebuilding factories. Sergei Eisenstein's last play, *Gas Masks*, was set in a factory and acted by factory workers, its content their everyday tasks. There was an industrial ballet called *Iron Foundries* with stylized imitation of the noise of machinery, and this was performed in Baku in 1922 using foghorns of the Caspian fleet, factory sirens, two batteries of artillery, machine guns and massed choirs. Proletkult was fully committed to the creation of an exclusively industrial, productional art. Its supporters in the art world, the futurists and later the constructivists, were to try to revolutionize architecture, town planning and stage design, to take art away from the museum and the canvas and put it on the street, and to make it utilitarian, an instrument with which to fashion the new society. Indeed, art was to be abolished as a separate discipline and was to merge with life. Reality, in the sense of rifles, tanks and cars, entered the theatre, constructivist stage sets replaced scenery, and the curtain was abolished. Artists decorated the streets for festivals, and, more practically, constructivists took art to the factories. Constructivism, as an art movement, started in the winter of 1920–1. Its adherents rejected all traditional art as bourgeois and called for artists to go into the factory with an approach based on communist ideas. They were to use concrete materials to aid a radical transformation of society. Vkhutemas (the higher state artistic and technical workshops) aimed to train highly qualified master artists to raise the quality of industrial output. New clothing and furniture designs and architectural plans resulted, although not very many got past the drawing-board stage (Lenin's tomb being one of the few that did).

One of the designs which never left the drawing-board, but which came to personify the vision of a new scientific and industrial age, was Tatlin's tower for the Third International, planned to straddle the river Neva in Petrograd. A utilitarian monument (it was to incorporate three conference centres, a radio mast and other scientific wonders), it was also, and was meant to be, a symbol, built of iron and glass to glorify the new age. Although futurists and constructivists claimed to represent communist art, neither Lenin nor Lunacharsky would allow them to dominate the art world. Other forms of modernism survived, and Malevich, Lissitsky and Chagall all served the new state in its early years. Narkompros provided a forum in which many styles and beliefs competed.

This was possible partly because Lenin and the top Bolshevik leaders regarded its activities as of secondary importance unless they affected politics. Neither Lenin nor Trotsky agreed with the left in giving priority to cultural issues. Both believed, with differing emphases, that politics and economics were fundamental in the struggle for socialism and that cultural change would come naturally later, and as a result of these changes. Trotsky, in *Literature and Revolution*, firmly rejected the idea of a separate proletarian culture. The eventual new culture would be classless and come about through economic transformation. Proletkult assumed that socialist art was immediately achievable, but Trotsky maintained that it would come only in the future and would be of a standard as yet unconsidered. In Trotsky's view the period of the civil war was inimical to art; only prosperity and abundance in the eventual socialist society would permit a herioc leap into a new artistic world for all humanity. Meanwhile all schools of art which were not hostile to the revolution should be tolerated. One historian has classified his ideas as 'revolutionary heroic' (McClelland, 1980, p. 408), and his messianic utterances have been noted. But his insistence on using military means to tackle the economic crisis was to have cultural implications. One such was in education, where a battle emerged by 1920 between Trotsky and Lunacharsky, who was committed to a broad cultural approach to schooling: egalitarian, polytechnic, and as far as possible the responsibility of the local soviets through the new united labour schools. Trotsky, by 1920, was advocating centralized, technical and vocational training, under military conditions. This, like other conflicts, was settled by Lenin, who supported party central control but backed Lunacharsky on a wider curriculum, albeit one with compulsory Marxism classes and bourgeois experts as teachers.

Lenin remained the most pragmatic in his attitude to cultural revolution and the most convinced of the primacy of politics and the party. As he commented to Lunacharsky in the midst of one of the arguments about Proletkult: '(1) Proletarian culture = communism; (2) it is carried out by the RCP [Russian Communist Party]; (3) the proletarian class = RCP = Soviet power. We are all agreed on this aren't we?' (*CW*, 1970, vol. 44, p. 445). For Lenin, nothing in the cultural field could be apolitical or outside the party. His own tastes were conservative. He much preferred Pushkin to Mayakovsky and saw no reason why, if the theatres and opera houses were made available to them, the working class should not appreciate the classics. He was concerned to establish party control over the press and over the cinema, an art form he esteemed highly, and with Nadezhda Krupskaya was deeply interested in education. But he viewed the cultural concerns of the left with hostility and suspicion. Above all, he assumed that the establishment of any new culture would take at least a generation and that it must assimilate the best of the old art. Once the initial phase of revolutionary iconoclasm was over, by mid-1918 he was concerned to set up museums and to requisition aristocratic palaces and confiscate art treasures. By the end of that year the new workers' state had nearly three times the number of museums that had been in existence before 1917.

There were, however, some fields in which his enthusiasm

saw no bounds. The abolition of money was one (in 1918), and electrification was another. Goelro, the State Electricity Trust, was created largely on Lenin's initiative, and one of his most famous slogans was to be 'Communism is soviet power plus the electrification of the whole country.' Another concern, one shared by all sides of the cultural and political spectrum, was the productivity of industry. All visions of the new society depended on abundance and thus increasing production levels. The Bolsheviks all assumed that the new proletarian society would continue to be based on large-scale machine industry, but that with the abolition of capitalism that industry would work for people and would cease to be an alienating force. Lenin had been interested in capitalist techniques for raising productivity since before the First World War, including those of the American, F. W. Taylor. Indeed, the American model was widely admired in early Soviet Russia. Bogdanov, by the years of the civil war, was working on what he called 'tektology', or a general organizational science of society which would submit the whole economy to one harmonious plan. Trotsky was to use Taylorist methods in the army, although Bogdanov vigorously attacked the militarization of lifestyle which would result. Bogdanov stressed the need for voluntary development by the workers themselves of new techniques which would guard against the dangers of an automated mass society. Many of his followers, however, saw the modern factory as a laboratory for a new science of work, where people, properly monitored and cared for, could develop a lifestyle synchronized to the rhythms of industry. A whole plethora of institutes, trade unions and academies grew up round what became known in Russia not as Taylorism but the Scientific Organization of Labour (NOT), and it became in itself part of the drive to create a new industrial collective society. For Lenin, however, it had a much more practical task. Calling for an end to the intellectual fantasies that enveloped the movement, he urged what he called 'the ABC of organization': 'Prove ... that you, the united proletariat ... are able to distribute

grain and coal in such a way as to husband every pood ...
that every pound of surplus grain and coal is ... supplied
to starving workers. ... This is the fundamental task of
"proletarian culture" of proletarian organisation' (*CW*,
1965, vol. 29, p. 374).

Thus the Bolshevik leaders disagreed considerably during
these years about how a new society was to be shaped and
what form that shape would take. Nevertheless, whether,
like Lenin, it was a concern primarily with educating the
proletariat to support the ideas of the new regime, or, as
was the case with supporters of either of the two left
wings of Bolshevism (the constructivist/industrial and the
spiritual/philosophical trends, we might call them), it was
a question of an immediate transformation of society, the
party was deeply involved in propaganda and education
over these years. The diversity and complexity of these
propaganda activities stemmed partly from the conflicts of
ideas and interests which have been explained above, but
also from an inherent belief in the interconnection between
different branches of art and between art and social life.
Artists like Mayakovsky consciously operated in several
fields – poster art, theatre, circus, film, mass pageants.

An enormous variety of experiments were tried out
during these years, and there was considerable confusion.
In the early years of the regime there were two distinct
problems for the enthusiastic builders of a new society: the
need to attack the old cultural heritage and to oppose the
remnants of the old regime – the Whites, the foreign
interventionists, the bourgeoisie and the church; and,
secondly, to present an alternative model for a socialist
society.

The first was relatively easy. Posters, films and theatre
satirized the old order with what Mayakovsky called
'formidable laughter'. Class hatred against the old exploiters
– the tsar, the church, the landlords, the capitalists – was
a constant theme. There was considerable iconoclasm
during the early months and years: statues were dismantled,

churches closed and defaced, palaces turned into workers' clubs.

One project in the very early months was specifically associated with Lenin himself. It was he who initiated the idea of monumental propaganda – the removal of statues of the old regime and their replacement with revolutionary heroes, both Russian and European. No living revolutionary was honoured, but the suggested names included many non-Marxists, such as Danton, Robespierre and Bakunin. Many left-wing intellectuals opposed the policy of erecting statues to individuals and advocated monuments glorifying workers, peasants and soldiers. In practice not many were actually constructed. Some were built by abstract artists and met with a hostile reception from the population. The Moscow Soviet refused to sanction the idea, but Lenin persisted for some months in encouraging it.*

New symbols and rituals were developed to replace pre-revolutionary ones. The imperial eagles were replaced by the hammer and sickle. Red flags replaced icons in processions. Saints' days and religious holidays were abolished as part of a determinedly atheistic and anticlerical campaign. Church holidays like Easter and Christmas were replaced by, or transformed into, socialist ones such as 1 May or, later, the date of Rosa Luxemburg's murder. Red weddings and Red baptisms replaced Christian celebrations, and new rituals accompanied them. Towns, streets and children were given new, revolutionary names. One favourite girl's name of the period was Ninel, which is Lenin spelt backwards.

There were several, not often successful, attempts by the followers of Alexandra Kollontai to abolish the nuclear family and to experiment with various schemes for communal living. Communes were set up in the countryside practising a strictly egalitarian lifestyle. Crêches and communal eating facilities were a feature of many new town-planning designs – although few were implemented. Accounts of such schemes, and the misreporting of Kollontai's ideas of 'free love' as meaning promiscuity, led to much hostile comment both in Russia and abroad. Lurid accounts of 'the collectivization of women' appeared in the western press. As Commissar of Social Welfare, Kollontai introduced laws to permit civil registration of marriage, easy divorce and the abolition of illegitimacy. More reluctantly she sanctioned abortion as a temporary necessity in revolutionary conditions, and large numbers of newly liberated women took advantage of the new laws. The new Women's Department of the Communist Party (Zhenotdel) worked hard to raise women's consciousness of their liberated role in the new society, and many women held prominent positions during the civil war. However, the family was more likely to break up through conscription into the army, easy divorce and lack of housing space than through conscious revolutionary experimentation.

In a largely semiliterate or illiterate society much stress was placed on visual propaganda: posters were everywhere, put out by large numbers of institutions – trade unions, commissariats and soviets – during the civil war. Artists were employed by different bodies, and styles varied considerably. Both style and content of posters were criticized in the press, and there was much argument over themes and effectiveness: on the advisability of using the technique and form of the pre-twentieth-century peasant woodcut, to put over a new message to the peasantry; on the use of allegory and symbolism (the portrayal of class enemies as monsters, for example); and on the acceptability of abstract art forms for political propaganda purposes.

Mass open-air spectacles, the Russian equivalent of the French revolutionary *journées*, were common and popular during the civil war. Celebrations of revolutionary events from Russian and European history, such as the Paris Commune and the eighteenth-century Russian peasant revolt under Pugachev, were carried out on their anniversaries. The most famous was the 'Restorming of the Winter Palace' on the third anniversary of the October revolution which used real guns, real tanks and a large part of the population of Petrograd. It re-enacted the events of 1917 with a 'White' stage and a 'Red' stage set up before the Winter Palace. The re-enactment caused considerable damage and was opposed by Lenin. Trotsky regarded it as out of place and frivolous. Many were hastily adapted folk epics or mystery plays. Mayakovsky's *150 million* set up huge puppet figures of Wilson, Lloyd George and Clemenceau. Wilson, symbol of capitalism, was opposed by Ivan, who, as in the old Russian fairy stories, when cut in two opened to show Red Army soldiers coming out of his wound. Mayakovsky's *Mystery Bouffe* was a good example of the adaptation technique – in this case the biblical story of the Flood. In the play, pairs of clean (bourgeois) and unclean (proletariat) build a new ark, and a man walks on the water, 'the most common or garden man', 'the indeflectible spirit of eternal evolution' who leads them both to heaven and to hell and finally to a new promised land on earth.

On May Day 1920 a spectacle called 'The Liberation of Labour' involved 20,000 people in Petrograd. The scene was set before a wall in the middle of which was a golden gate. From behind the gate came music, light and colour, symbolizing freedom, equality and fraternity. In front of it stood cannon, guards and slaves. A procession of rulers and oppressors from Byzantine emperors to top-hatted bourgeoisie passed by. A series of popular revolts – those of Spartacus and Pugachev, the French revolution – were portrayed as attacks on the gate, and all were beaten off until the Red Army marched in; the gate flew open and the kingdom of peace was proclaimed by the playing of the *Internationale* and the letting off of fireworks.

Such displays ensured mass participation in a collective celebration of mass action which was also a practical education in revolutionary history. The tradition of such mass pageants was continued by Eisenstein in his early films. *Strike*, *Battleship Potemkin* and *October* (made in the mid-1920s) were all celebrations of revolutionary history, putting forward the same lessons as the civil war events and posters: the role of the masses, internationalism, class struggle and a simple black (or red) and white picture of historical events. None used professional actors, and the films were made by the citizens of Odessa or Leningrad. Over 11,000 people took part in the making of *October* in 1927, and that was only one of several anniversary films made that year.

Mass events of this nature were one way of involving large numbers of people. Others were fictional trials – of White generals, priests or political figures from western Europe. The conventional theatre also went out to the people as well as adapting its own productions to include revolutionary messages and new 'open theatre' acting techniques. Theatre clubs were established in factories and army barracks. Before the First World War, both Mayakovsky and the theatre producer V. Meyerhold had been involved in attempts to take theatre based on the traditions of circus and fairground puppet shows into the streets and the villages. In the civil war years this tradition was to be expanded. Music hall and circus traditions were adapted to put over the revolutionary appeal. Proletkult had a department to train its actors in acrobatics and clowning. Decorated agit-trains and boats took acting troupes and propaganda material round the countryside. Travelling theatre groups performed at country railway stations or from trucks in village streets. There were only fifty village cinemas before 1925 but over 900 travelling cinema companies. Village theatre groups rewrote Pushkin's stories or peasant legends with a modern ending. They produced short, comic, anti-religious or anti-kulak pieces. There were short plays on electrification, on the evils of drink and on superstition. Rosta, the Russian telegraph agency, for which Mayakovsky worked, put out wall-posters using the strip-cartoon style of the old peasant woodcut, to argue for recruitment into the Red Army, for inoculation against cholera and for the diversification of crops.

Despite the emphasis on class struggle and the mass or proletarian initiative in building a new society, there was also, throughout the civil war years, a growing cult of

Lenin as hero. The old imperial porcelain factory put out statuettes of Bolshevik leaders, and Lenin especially became the subject of folk art and adoration. Gorky talked of him as a culture hero or man-god, possessed of superhuman abilities. Although Lenin himself discouraged the growing cult, not all his followers did so, and it achieved considerable proportions before his death.

It is very difficult to evaluate the success of the propaganda in changing people's attitudes or in bestowing legitimacy on the new regime. As the civil war ended and the foreign interventionists withdrew, it was clear that the new society had not been established. Many who were involved in the artistic experiments of those years were intellectuals and failed to produce images which were intelligible to the masses. There are many stories like that of the woman who, looking at a futurist statue of Bakunin, said in horror, 'they want us to pray to the devil', or of the peasant woman who crossed herself as she filed round Lenin's tomb in 1924. Despite the work of the Women's Department of the party (Zhenotdel) after 1919 it remained true that Bolshevik support was lower among women than among men, and lower in the countryside. As Trotsky was to comment, it was increasingly obvious that the political and even the economic tasks of the party were going to be easier to attain than that of creating a new man and a new lifestyle. Even enthusiasts were beginning to accept that the proletariat was not yet ready to enter the brave new world. It would indeed take decades and would have to be tackled from the bottom up. Trotsky, in his *Problems of Everyday Life*, put the emphasis on more mundane and basic changes in the creation of what has been called a social charter – basic literacy schemes (illiteracy actually increased during the period), and sermons against alcoholism, lateness, dirt and bad language. As the New Economic Policy marked a return to a money economy and reintroduced elements of capitalism into Soviet life, the artists of the civil war years found themselves turning their hands to advertising slogans. As Bukharin was to comment, 1921 was the year which saw the end of many illusions.

Conclusion

The Tenth Party Congress signalled not just the end of the civil war but in many ways the end of the revolution. By March 1921 the Communist Party controlled most of the territory of the old Russian empire. Finland, Poland, the Baltic states and Bessarabia were lost to it, and some outlying areas remained to be consolidated, but the Crimea was conquered, and, in the Ukraine, Makhno was driven into exile once his usefulness against the Whites was over. Georgia was incorporated by more subtle means. A treaty signed with the Menshevik government of Georgia in May 1920 recognized Georgian independence with the proviso that the small Georgian Communist Party be given freedom of action. The Georgian Communists then called on Moscow for aid, and the Red Army reached Tbilisi in February 1921 and ended Menshevik Georgia. 'Great Russian chauvinist' methods during the occupation and the treatment of the Georgian Communists led to conflict between Lenin and Stalin, his Commissar for Nationalities, the following year. By 1922 the Soviet Union was formally created as a Soviet Socialist Federal Republic.

But success in the civil war merely highlighted economic collapse and popular discontent at home and made it urgent that disagreements over how to proceed in peacetime be settled at the Tenth Party Congress. Behind debates about whether labour armies or an All-Russian Congress of Producers was the best way ahead lay more serious differences over what the revolution stood for – economic centralization or workers' control; one-party rule or socialist democracy – and how far these opposites could be reconciled.

The congress met in the shadow of the Kronstadt rebellion which, originating as it did from one of the bastions of soviet power, had concentrated wonderfully the minds of the party faithful. The Kronstadt experiment in soviet democracy had ended by July 1918 with the imposition of Bolshevik rule. Many Kronstadt leaders joined the party, and Red Kronstadt's support during the civil war was undeniable. Grassroots democratic organizations were closed, and party commissars and the new Political Department of the Baltic Fleet ran the naval base, but the argument that the Communist Party was the only possible representative of the working class and that all other parties were counter-revolutionary failed to win support. With the end of the civil war and with the increasing awareness by the relatively prosperous sailors of the plight of the countryside, discontent at the rule of the new commissars led to revolt.

Kronstadt openly returned to its 1917 programme of 'All Power to Soviets and not to Parties'. A large meeting in Anchor Square on 1 March 1921 adopted a resolution calling for trade-union autonomy, for freedom of speech and of the press for 'workers and peasants, anarchists and left socialist parties' (Getzler, 1983, pp. 213–14) and for new, multi-party elections to the soviets with secret ballots. Abolition of Chekas, labour armies, political departments and Communist Party military units were demanded on the grounds that 'no single party should have special privileges in the propaganda of its ideas' (ibid., p. 214). For Lenin, one of the most disturbing features was the near-total collapse of the local communists, and many recent converts now left the party to re-emerge as non-party leaders. A. Lamanov, who had been chairman of the Kronstadt soviet in 1917, was one of these, and as editor of the new *Izvestiya* he was to argue in print that the true soviet revolution of October 1917 had been usurped by a one-party dictatorship. Kronstadt's hope was for a third revolution, which would oust the commissars through the ballot box, and return to a truly soviet republic of toilers.

Although in private Lenin recognized what the revolt was about, in public it was described as a White Guard, SR plot and a counter-revolution. To have recognized that the sailors' grievances were the result of genuine disillusionment with the progress of the revolution would have involved questioning the validity of one-party rule and the vanguard role of the Communist Party. This Lenin was not prepared to do. Food supplies were hastily rushed to Petrograd to minimize the possibility of support, and the Red Army moved in. By 18 March the revolt was suppressed and Lamanov and hundreds of others were executed. At the Tenth Party Congress Lenin compromised. Many of Kronstadt's economic demands were granted. Labour armies were abolished, and requisition of grain was replaced by a tax in kind. The New Economic Policy, which allowed a free market in goods and even hiring of labour and limited renting of land, was agreed to with little debate by a confused and frightened party. Trotsky's hopes for a militarized road to socialism were over. If concessions were granted in the economy, however, Lenin coupled these with a clampdown on all opposition.

The Mensheviks and SRs, banned in practice from 1918, were now formally outlawed, and the trial of the SRs, the first show trial in Soviet history, was to follow the next year. Above all, Lenin used Kronstadt to defeat the Worker's Opposition. Although the leaders of the Workers' Opposition were among the most ardent opponents of Kronstadt, regarding freedom of opposition as possible only within the party, not between parties, Lenin drew the obvious and convenient conclusion that all opposition should be prohibited as 'harmful and impermissible'. The congress dutifully passed two resolutions – one on party unity and one specifically condemning the ideas of the Workers' Opposition as an 'anarcho-syndicalist deviation' and 'radically wrong in theory' (*CW*, 1965, vol. 32, pp. 245–6).

Kollontai and Shlyapnikov were still defining socialism in terms of open and free political debate within the party and, outside it, wide workers' participation, discussion and self-government through trade unions, soviets and a variety of elected class bodies. Against this stress on the workers creating socialism through their own efforts, Lenin again placed his emphasis firmly on the vanguard role of the party as educator. 'Marxism teaches', he wrote in one of his draft resolutions for the congress, 'that only the political party of the working class, i.e. the Communist Party, is capable of uniting, training and organizing a vanguard of the proletariat and the whole mass of the working people' against the 'inevitable petty bourgeois vacillations of this mass', and preventing it from relapsing into craft unionism and petty-bourgeois traditions (ibid., p. 246). Lenin's definition of revolution, even in 1917 when he placed most emphasis on popular participation, precluded what Kollontai saw as essential for the development of socialism – the development under communist political rule of a free, democratic and participatory civil society.

With the defeat of the Workers' Opposition and the suppression of Kronstadt, any such definition of soviet democracy within the Russian revolution ended. There were misgivings at the congress, but the appeal to party unity was a powerful one at such a time, and the party was used to Lenin's getting his own way. Karl Radek was reported as saying: 'let the Central Committee even be mistaken; that is less dangerous than the wavering which is now observable' (Schapiro, 1984, p. 199). 'My party, right or wrong' became an accepted attitude. The party now stood for a higher cause than individual freedom. It was a small step from this position to the dilemma which was to face Bukharin and Radek himself, among others, by the 1930s, when during the purge trials they were forced to choose between loyalty to their beliefs and loyalty to their party – a dilemma which is portrayed so graphically by the fictionalized 'old Bolshevik' Rubashov in Arthur Koestler's novel *Darkness at Noon*.

Glossary

CEC	All-Russian Central Executive Committee of Soviets
Cheka	All-Russian Extraordinary Commission for Combating Counter-Revolution and Sabotage (Bolshevik political police)
Comintern	Third International
Duma	Russian Parliament 1906–17
duma	elected town council
Goelro	State Electricity Trust
kombedy	poor peasant committees
komuch	SR re-establishment of the Constituent Assembly
kulak	rich peasant
Narkompros	Commissariat of the Enlightenment
Okhrana	tsarist political police
Orgburo	Organizational Bureau of the Central Committee
Politburo	Political Bureau of the Central Committee
pood	weight equivalent to 36 lb
Proletkult	proletarian culture movement
rabfak	workers' faculty: adult education class to raise students to university level
Rada	Ukrainian Government 1917–18
Rosta	Russian telegraph agency
soviet	elected workers' council
Sovnarkom	Council of People's Commissars
starosta	village or factory elder
Tsektran	Transport Commission
Vesenkha	Supreme Economic Council
Vikzhel	All-Russian railway union

vkhutemas	higher state artistic and technical workshops
volost	rural district
zemlyachestvo	mutual-aid organization founded in factories by peasants from the same village or area
zemstvo	local government body founded 1864
Zhenotdel	Women's Department of the Communist Party

POLITICAL MOVEMENTS

Anarchism. The name given to a phase of nineteenth-century revolutionary socialism associated with P.-J. Proudhon (1809–65) and M. Bakunin (1814–76), which denied the need for any form of government in a society. The anarchists' ideal was complete individual autonomy, but many also believed in a collectivist lifestyle. There were several groups of anarchists active in the Russian revolution: anarcho-individualists, anarcho-communists and anarcho-syndicalists. The first two groups preached violent revolutionary action against all forms of private property and the state. They believed all government was evil, including a revolutionary government, and, although they collaborated with the Bolsheviks during 1917, they broke with them after October and went into opposition. Their vision of the revolution was of a loose association of voluntary organizations which would rise spontaneously once the bourgeois state was destroyed.

Populism. Russian revolutionary movement from 1860 to the 1880s, influenced by utopian socialist and anarchist ideas. Hostile to any strong central state, populists advocated a decentralist and federalist society. They preached a form of rural socialism based on the peasant commune and believed that Russia could pass directly from feudalism to socialism, bypassing the capitalist phase. Some populists established conspiratorial groups and practised terrorism, but the majority believed in 'going to the people' and spreading socialist ideas among the peasantry. The belief in decentralism and local self-government influenced Mensheviks and left-wing Kadets, and the conspiratorial groups influenced Lenin's idea of the party; but it was the SRs who most closely continued the populist tradition at the time of the revolution.

Syndicalism. A movement which developed in France in the 1880s after the failure of the Paris Commune. It combined the anarchist distrust of the state and political action with a belief in trade-union power. Anarcho-syndicalists advocated direct action by the workers to overthrow capitalism through a general strike, and aimed at a new social order based on producers' communes, workers' self-management, trade unions and profit-sharing. Syndicalist ideas had some influence over the trade-union movement in Russia from 1905 and among left-wing Bolsheviks, including both the Workers' Opposition and followers of Bogdanov.

RUSSIAN POLITICAL PARTIES IN 1917

Liberal and right-wing parties:

Constitutional Democrats (Kadets). Established in October 1905 as a parliamentary party. Programme of civil liberties and a full British-type parliamentary constitution, but of a very radical kind, including universal suffrage.

Union of 17 October (Octobrists). Established after the granting of the October Manifesto in 1905 to work with the imperial regime to implement the promises of the manifesto. A conservative centre party committed to gradual reform.

Progressists. Founded in 1912 as a mouthpiece of industrial and commercial groups in the fourth Duma.

Socialist parties:

Socialist Revolutionary Party (SRs). Heirs to the ideas of the populist movement. Founded in 1901 as an openly revolutionary and terrorist party. It built up a wide following among peasants after 1905, but its radical programme also appealed to the new working class.

Left SRs. Broke away to form a separate party in October 1917, and collaborated with the Bolsheviks. Members of Sovnarkom from December 1917 to March 1918.

SR Maximalists. A left-wing splinter group which broke from the SR party in 1904.

Trudoviks (Labour Group). Formed from peasant delegates to the first Duma. On the moderate wing of the SR party.

Marxists (Russian Social Democratic Labour Party). Founded in 1898 and split at the Second Congress in 1903 into a radical *Bolshevik* (majority) wing and a more moderate *Menshevik* (minority) one.

Bolsheviks. Became a separate party in 1912 and changed their name to the *Communist Party* in March 1918. Although the Bolshevik party did not formally split, a left-wing opposition to Lenin existed before 1917 under the influence of Bogdanov. *Left Communists* were a group round Bukharin who opposed the treaty of Brest-Litovsk in the spring of 1918.

Mensheviks. Closer to the German Social Democrats in their belief in the necessity for a two-stage revolution and a long period of bourgeois liberal government before socialism could be established.

Menshevik Internationalists. Led by Martov, this was a left-wing Menshevik group in 1917 which supported Lenin's anti-war stance and by October believed that the Petrograd Soviet should assume power.

Interdistrict Group. Supporters of Trotsky who joined the Bolsheviks during the summer of 1917.

'Moderate Socialists'. Refers to the right-wing SRs and Mensheviks who led the Petrograd Soviet from February to September 1917 and who joined the coalition government in May.

Chronology

Dates old-style until 1/14 February 1918, when Russia adopted the western (Gregorian) calendar; thereafter new-style.

1914	*1 Aug.*	Russia declares war on Germany.
1917	*18 Feb.*	Strike begins at the Putilov works.
	23	Workers demonstrate in Petrograd.
	25	General strike.
	26	Nicholas II dissolves the Duma.
	27	Establishment of unofficial committee of the Duma. Establishment of Executive Committee of the Petrograd Soviet.
	1 March	Order No. 1. First factory committee established in Petrograd.
	2	Nicholas II abdicates and Provisional Government formed.
	10	Agreement between Petrograd Soviet and employers on eight-hour day and recognition of factory committees.
	12	Stalin and Kamenev return to Petrograd.
	3 Apr.	Lenin returns to Petrograd.
	4	*April Theses* delivered.
	7	Vikzhel established.
	18	Milyukov's Note to the Allies.
	20–21	Demonstrations against Milyukov.
	30	Resignation of Guchkov.
	2 May	Resignation of Milyukov.

4	Trotsky returns to Petrograd.
4–28	All-Russian Congress of Peasant Deputies.
5	Formation of first coalition government.
27–30	Elections to Petrograd city *duma*. Moderate socialists win.
30 May–3 June	First conference of factory committees.
3–24 June	First All-Russian Congress of Workers' and Soldiers' Soviets.
10	Bolsheviks call off planned anti-war demonstration.
18	Military offensive begins. Soviet-organized demonstration in Petrograd.
25	Elections to Moscow city *duma*. SR win.
2 July	Ukrainian crisis. Resignation of Kadets from coalition government.
3–4	July Days.
5–6	Bolsheviks arrested and presses closed. Lenin flees to Finland.
8	Kerensky becomes Premier.
18	Kornilov appointed commander-in-chief.
23	Trotsky under arrest. (Freed 4 September.)
24	Second coalition formed.
26 July–3 Aug.	Bolsheviks' Sixth Party Congress.
12–15 Aug.	State Conference in Moscow.
21	Riga occupied by the Germans.
26–30	The Kornilov affair.
1 Sept.	Kornilov arrested. Republic proclaimed.
9	Bolshevik majority in the Petrograd Soviet.
14–22	Democratic Conference.
15	Bolshevik Central Committee rejects Lenin's call for an armed insurrection.

24 Sept.	Elections to Moscow city *duma*. Bolshevik success.
25	Third coalition formed.
7 Oct.	Lenin returns to Petrograd in disguise.
10	Bolshevik Central Committee agrees to prepare for armed insurrection.
11	Zinoviev and Kamenev circulate their objections.
12	Petrograd Soviet establishes the Military Revolutionary Committee.
17	CEC of Petrograd Soviet postpones convocation of the Second Congress from 20 to 25 October.
17–23	First All-Russian Conference of Factory Committees.
24	Provisional Government takes counter-measures against MRC. Lenin arrives in Smolny (Bolshevik HQ).
24–25	Bolsheviks take control of the city.
25	Kerensky leaves Winter Palace. Government arrested that night. Second Congress of Soviets opens 10.40 p.m.
26	Establishment of Sovnarkom. Establishment of the Committee for the Salvation of the Fatherland and the Revolution, by moderate socialists.
29	Vikzhel threatens railway strike.
30	Krasnov defeated.
30 Oct.–3 Nov.	Inter-party talks regarding coalition.
4 Nov.	Resignation of Kamenev and Zinoviev.
7	Rada proclaims the Ukraine an independent republic.
8	Decree on Land. Decree on Peace.

10–25 Nov.	Extraordinary Congress of Peasant Deputies.
_12_	Elections to the Constituent Assembly.
_14_	Decree on Workers' Control. Talks begin at Brest-Litovsk.
_28_	Kadet party outlawed.
1 Dec	Establishment of Vesenkha.
_2_	Armistice signed at Brest-Litovsk.
_7_	Establishment of Cheka.
_12_	Left SRs join Sovnarkom.
_14_	Decree nationalizing banks.
1918 _5–6 Jan._	Constituent Assembly meets and is dispersed.
_11_	Central Committee accepts Trotsky's 'neither war nor peace' formula.
_15_	Decree establishing the Red Army.
_15–16_	Abortive Bolshevik rising against the Rada government in Kiev.
1/14 Feb.	Adoption of western (Gregorian) calendar, which was thirteen days in advance of the Russian one.
_18_	German troops advance and Bolsheviks accept peace terms.
_19_	Decree on the Socialisation of Land.
3 Mar.	Treaty of Brest-Litovsk.
_6–8_	Bolsheviks' Seventh Party Congress.
_12_	Government moved to Moscow.
_15_	Left SRs leave Sovnarkom.
_16_	Trotsky appointed Commissar for War.
5 Apr.	Allied ships land at Murmansk.
_13_	Kornilov killed in action. Bolshevik drive against anarchists in Moscow and elsewhere.
_29_	Germans establish puppet government in the Ukraine under Skoropadsky.

	14 May	Czech–Soviet incident on the Trans-Siberian railway at Chelyabinsk.
	25	Czech legion controls Trans-Siberian railway.
	8 June	SR government established at Samara.
	11	Establishment of *kombedy*.
	6 July	Left SRs assassinate German ambassador, Count Mirbach.
	8	SR uprising at Yaroslavl.
	16	Murder of tsar and members of the royal family at Ekaterinburg.
	2 Aug.	British land at Archangel and establish anti-Bolshevik government.
	30	Lenin wounded. Red terror formally established.
	10 Sept.	Red Army captures Kazan.
	23	Directorate established at Ufa.
	8 Oct.	Red Army captures Samara.
	9	Directorate moves to Omsk.
	11 Nov.	Armistice signed between Germany and the Allies.
	18	Kolchak assumes supreme power in Omsk.
	14 Dec.	Collapse of Skoropadsky regime in the Ukraine.
	17	French land at Odessa.
1919	6 Feb.	Red Army occupies Kiev.
	15	Denikin assumes supreme command on the south-east front.
	2–7 Mar.	First Congress of the Comintern.
	18–23	Eighth Party Congress.
	8 Apr.	French evacuate Odessa.
	10	Red Army invades the Crimea.
	4 June	Makhno's mutiny against the Bolsheviks.
	31 Aug.	Denikin occupies Kiev.
	27 Sept.	Allies evacuate Archangel.
	14 Oct.	Denikin captures Orel.

	20 Oct.	Red Army retakes Orel.
	22	Yudenich reaches suburbs of Petrograd.
	14 Nov.	Yudenich defeated.
	16 Dec.	Red Army captures Kiev.
1920	15 Jan.	Capture of Kolchak by Bolsheviks.
	7 Feb.	Execution of Kolchak.
	29 Mar–5 Apr.	Ninth Party Congress.
	4 Apr.	Denikin succeeded by Wrangel.
	24	Outbreak of Russo-Polish war.
	6 May	Polish forces occupy Kiev.
	6 June	Wrangel launches offensive.
	12	Red Army reoccupies Kiev.
	17 Aug.	Polish counter-offensive.
	12 Oct.	Russo-Polish provisional peace treaty.
	14 Nov.	Wrangel evacuates the Crimea.
	26	Red Army drive against Makhno.
1921	16 Feb.	Red Army invades Georgia.
	1 Mar.	Kronstadt revolt.
	8–16	Tenth Party Congress.

Guide to Further Reading

See also the works listed as References.

Anweiler, O. 1974: *The Soviets*. New York.
Atkinson, D. 1983: *The End of the Russian Land Commune 1905–1930*. Stanford, Cal.
Carr, E. H. 1950–3: *The Bolshevik Revolution*. 3 vols. London.
Carr, E. H. 1979: *The Russian Revolution from Lenin to Stalin 1917–29*. London.
Chamberlin, W. H. 1931: *The Russian Revolution 1917–21*. 2 vols. New York.
Cohen, S. F. 1973: *Bukharin and the Bolshevik Revolution: A Political Biography 1888–1938*. New York.
Crisp, O. 1976: *Studies in the Russian Economy before 1914*. London.
Daniels, R. V. 1967: *Red October*. London.
Ferro, M. 1972: *The Russian Revolution of February 1917*. London.
Ferro, M. 1980: *October 1917*. London.
Fitzpatrick, S. 1970: *The Commissariat of the Enlightenment*. Cambridge.
Fitzpatrick, S. 1982: *The Russian Revolution*. Oxford.
Fülöp-Miller, R. 1929: *The Mind and Face of Bolshevism*. New York.
Gleason, A., Kenez P., and Stites R. (eds) 1985: *Bolshevik Culture*. Indiana.
Harding, N. 1981: *Lenin's Political Thought*, vol. 2. London.
Hasegawa, T. 1981: *The February Revolution in Petrograd 1917*. Seattle.
Hosking, G. 1985: *A History of the Soviet Union*. London.

Katkov, G. 1967: *Russia 1917: The February Revolution*. London.

Katkov, G. 1980: *The Kornilov Affair*. London.

Keep, J. L. H. 1976: *The Russian Revolution: A Study in Mass Mobilisation*. London.

Knei-Paz, B. 1978: *The Social and Political Thought of Leon Trotsky*. Oxford.

Kochan, L. 1966: *Russia in Revolution 1890–1918*. London.

Liebman, M. 1975: *Leninism under Lenin*. London.

Lieven, D. C. B. 1983: *Russia and the Origins of the First World War*. London.

McCauley, M. 1981: *The Soviet Union since 1917*. London.

McKean, R. B. 1977: *The Russian Constitutional Monarchy*. London.

Malle, S. 1985: *The Economic Organisation of War Communism 1918–21*. Cambridge.

Mandel, D. 1983: *The Petrograd Workers and the Fall of the Old Regime*. London.

Mandel, D. 1984: *The Petrograd Workers and the Soviet Seizure of Power*. London.

Mawdsley, E. 1978: *The Russian Revolution and the Baltic Fleet*. London.

Nove, A. 1969: *An Economic History of the USSR*. London.

Pearson, R. 1977: *The Russian Moderates and the Crisis of Tsarism*. London.

Pipes, R. (ed.) 1968: *Revolutionary Russia*. Cambridge, Mass.

Polan, A. J. 1984: *Lenin and the End of Politics*. London.

Rabinowitch, A. 1968: *Prelude to Revolution: The Petrograd Bolsheviks and the July 1917 Uprising*. Indiana.

Rabinowitch, A. 1976: *The Bolsheviks Come to Power*. New York.

Rigby, T. H. 1979: *Lenin's Government: Sovnarkom 1917–22*. Cambridge.

Rosenberg, W. G. 1974: *Liberals in the Russian Revolution*. Princeton, NJ.

Rosenberg, W. G. (ed.) 1984: *Bolshevik Visions: First Phase of the Cultural Revolution in Soviet Russia*. Ann Arbor, Mich.

Schapiro, L. 1966: *The Communist Party of the Soviet Union*. London.

Service, R. 1986: *The Russian Revolution 1900–27*. London.

Suny, R. G. 1972: *The Baku Commune*. Princeton, NJ.

Ulam, A. 1969: *Lenin and the Bolsheviks*. London.

Wade, R. A. 1969: *The Russian Search for Peace February–October 1917*. Stanford, Cal.

References

Bone, A. (ed.) 1974: *The Bolsheviks and the October Revolution: Minutes of the Central Committee of the Russian RSDLP (bolsheviks) Aug. 1917–Feb. 1918.* London.

Bukharin, N., and Preobrazhensky, E. 1969: *The ABC of Communism*, ed. E. H. Carr. London.

Bunyan, J., and Fisher, H. (eds) 1934: *The Bolshevik Revolution: Documents.* New York.

Daniels, R. V. 1960: *The Conscience of the Revolution.* Cambridge, Mass.

Denikin, A. I. 1921: *Ocherki Russkoi Smuty.* 2 vols. Paris.

Getzler, I. 1983: *Kronstadt 1917–21: The Fate of a Soviet Democracy.* Cambridge.

Gill, G. 1979: *Peasants and Government in the Russian Revolution.* London.

Golder, F. A. (ed.) 1927: *Documents of Russian History 1914–17.* New York.

Holt, A. (ed.) 1977: *Alexandra Kollontai: Selected Writings.* London.

Keep, J. (ed.) 1979: *The Debate on Soviet Power.* Oxford.

Koenker, D. 1981: *Moscow Workers and the 1917 Revolution.* Princeton, NJ.

Leggett, G. 1981: *The Cheka: Lenin's Political Police.* Oxford.

Lenin, V. I. 1960–70: *Collected Works.* 4th edn. Moscow.

McCauley, M. (ed.) 1975: *The Russian Revolution and the Soviet State 1917–21: Documents.* London.

McClelland, J. C. 1980: Utopianism versus revolutionary heroism in Bolshevik policy: the proletarian culture debate. *Slavic Review* (September 1980), 403–25.

Mgebrov, A. 1929: *Zhizn v Teatre.* 2 vols. Moscow.

Milyukov, P. N. 1921: *Istoriya Vtoroi Russkoi Revoliutsii*. 2 vols. Sofia.

Reed, J. 1960: *Ten Days that Shook the World*. New York.

Riha, T. 1969: *A Russian European*. Notre Dame.

Roobol, W. H. 1976: *Tsereteli: A Democrat in the Russian Revolution*. The Hague.

Schapiro, L. 1984: *1917*. Harmondsworth.

Scheibert, P. 1971: Lenin, Bogdanov and the concept of proletarian culture. In B. W. Eissenstat (ed.) *Lenin and Leninism, State Law and Society*. Lexington.

Serge, V. 1963: *Memoirs of a Revolutionary 1901–41*. Oxford.

Serge, V. 1972: *Year One of the Russian Revolution*. London.

Service, R. 1979: *The Bolshevik Party in Revolution: A Study in Organisational Change 1917–23*. London.

Smith, S. A. 1983: *Red Petrograd*. Cambridge.

Steinberg, I. N. 1930: *Souvenirs d'un commissaire du peuple*. Paris.

Sukhanov, N. N. 1955: *The Russian Revolution of 1917: A Personal Record*. Oxford.

Thomson, B. 1972: *The Premature Revolution: Russian Literature and Society 1917–46*. London.

Trotsky, L. 1921: *The Defence of Terrorism (Terrorism and Communism)*. London.

Trotsky, L. 1934: *The History of the Russian Revolution*. 2 vols. Sofia.

Trotsky, L. 1960: *Literature and Revolution*. Ann Arbor, Mich.

Tyrkova-Williams, A. 1919: *From Liberty to Brest-Litovsk*. London.

Voline, V. 1974: *The Unknown Revolution*. Montreal.

Wildman, A. 1980: *The End of the Russian Imperial Army*. Princeton, NJ.

Index

Index by Keith Seddon